I PROMISE I'M WORTHY

Emma Appleton

Michael Terence
Publishing

First published in paperback by
Michael Terence Publishing in 2020
www.mtp.agency

ISBN 9781913653071

All the names in this book have been changed, including that of the
author, to ensure her safety. The events described took place in the late
1970s and 1980s. Most of the people mentioned are still alive.

Cover image
Emma Appleton

Cover design

*Dedicated to my children, grandchildren and to Russ,
my angel in the sky.*

Contents

1:

There's No Place Like Home

Nothing mattered to me apart from being touched. I'd wait all day to feel the warm feelings that no one could give me but them. I enjoyed it – I felt great – it was a beautiful feeling having a wet vagina. It used to be in my head all day. I wonder what's going to happen tonight – I wish I had this feeling all the time. I wish I felt like this when I was away from them. I wanted everyone to give me that feeling – that feeling of love that was so overwhelming, the feeling that no one could love you more than this and this is how they showed you. Touching, feeling, needing, wanting, wanting that love over and over again, needing to feel the compassion, the desire. It overwhelmed me. I liked how it felt. I wanted more – it was the most beautiful thing, the closeness – the feeling that you were so special, so loved. I was beautiful. I was put up on a pedestal and this was how life was meant to be.

Everything was about sex – I needed, wanted and had to have it. I didn't care who from – I was getting enough at home – but the desire grew through me and it wouldn't stop. Yes, please to anyone. I can do that – not a problem. You want me to suck your dick, you want me to bend over, not a problem, you're welcome. I was 10 years old! You can have me any way you want because it was normal. I was having sexual thoughts when I was five and was a predator by nine so if you want to impress me with – you are beautiful, you are a good person, you are everything I've ever wanted – you're wasting your time. I've heard that since I was born. No one really means what they say, no one is genuine, no one loves you. It's all about what people take. They take and take from you until you end up like this, 45 years old – crisis team, psychologists, psychiatrists, tablets, therapy. When you have a traffic queue of memories in your head and you must let it out and the only way you can do it, is to write it down. To hope someone feels the same, to hope you're not on your own. To want to be normal – I've never been normal. I've always been clever. No one can hurt what they can't see. I'm like a chameleon – I can change to whoever you want me to be. You want fun, I'm there, you want to be loved, I'm there, you want to shout, I'll listen.

You, you, you, you, never about me because if you looked and tried to see what's inside of me it would hurt you, would disappoint you. I'm the biggest fuck-up you will ever see. But I won't let you see that because I'm clever. Let me introduce you to my mask. The mask I've worn since I was five – the mask I built to protect myself, the mask that has just fallen off. I did a good job for 45 years but one little thing was the tipping point – one thing I never imagined would turn my life upside down – a man!! But it wasn't about the man – I've had many of those – it was the rejection. Rejected again and again and again but the last one tipped me over the edge, the last one I trusted and believed in. I had my castle and its walls and the moat that I'd built that surrounded me, my safe zone. He took it apart layer by layer until I felt safe. I belonged, somewhere I was needed. I was loved. Finally, I was safe, but he rejected me and that was my tipping point. I felt unworthy, I was useless, I was nothing and no matter that for all those years my mask was my saviour, it disappeared in a second, in a ruthless text message. I didn't know what was happening – this person I'd been for so long – the one that was full of life and energy. I couldn't smile, I lost all respect for myself and then everything came flooding back, Pandora's box was open and I couldn't shut it, thought after thought, trauma after trauma, everything I'd locked away, hitting me, slapping me in the face. Reality, pain, hurt, everything I didn't want to think about was just there terrorising my thoughts. I'd tipped, I broke and I was back there again – back to being five years old – reliving everything that happened from that moment. I was awake in my own nightmare. Sink or swim time – and I sank.

My first memory was being a princess – a beauty queen walking around in my beautiful dress, hair in ringlets. I must have been four or five, staying up late for my mum to do my hair for the next day, wrapping each strand of hair around her finger, pulling my head to and fro, wrapping them in clips that I'd have to sleep in all night. My mother was obsessed with us being beautiful, myself and my two sisters. Now I realise why! It was her control – how everyone would perceive her as a loving mother, buying her children the best clothes, the best shoes, having the best cars, dressed up for us to sit on the bonnets and parade around the streets. Look at Maggie's kids – aren't they beautiful? What a wonderful mum she is!

Being a princess had its downside too because the nicer you looked the more you would have someone's fingers inside you. I couldn't sleep all night before a competition because my head hurt from all the pins in it and the day of the competition, I'd have my make – up done. I was told to smile and look sweet, sit on the car bonnet and my reward was getting fingered when it finished by Michael Pyre in the back of the car on my way home. Michael was my mother's friend – I remember the thick rims of his glasses. He was around 5ft, a skinny man and looked very old to me but I was four or five so being fifteen was old to me then. He was my first experience of being rewarded for being a good girl. Something that became the norm in my life.

I don't remember how I felt at the time – I was a child and it was normal for me; you get taught things as you're growing up that become a part of your everyday life. My parents split up when I was a newborn. I can't tell you how long they were together – I don't know. I know I couldn't see what my dad looked like because in all the pictures my mother had, his head was cut out. He was having an affair with the babysitter whilst my mother was pregnant with me. My eldest sister, Sharon, told me my dad used to go fishing and leave the maggots in the fridge – that's one of the two memories she has of him. She told me my mother put me on the doorstep when she brought me back from hospital because she blamed me for her getting fat and that's why my dad had an affair. I think that was the start of our loveless relationship. I think she hated me – wanted to punish me for her losing my dad when in reality the babysitter was 20 years younger and my dad couldn't keep his dick in his pants. Apparently, he liked a drink and Sharon said when my mum went to work, my dad, and I use that word loosely, used to lock my sisters outside so he could sleep with the babysitter.

None of this I remember – I just remember Sean. I thought he was my dad. When I was young, all I knew was him. He used to take us to the Wimpy and the Little Chef and KFC. I started Morris Dancing and he used to take us and always afterwards to one of those places for tea which was a big treat back then. The Little Chef has other memories later in life, but I wanted to go back there because of the memories – as a child, they were happy times. On special occasions, he used to take us to the Britannia in Manchester. Him and my mum had Irish coffees and he used to get us one with no alcohol in, so they looked the same. I can't say if my mum and Sean were in a relationship because I never saw them kissing or hugging or holding hands. He was just around, and I thought he was just meant to be there. He used to take me horse riding. I believed it was my horse – he was called Danny and I loved him so much. He was so old, but I could talk to him like I talked to all the animals we had later. They were my escape – the animals and the garden.

Sean rang the house one day. I'll never forget it – we had a grey telephone in the hallway. I answered. He said I can't come to see you anymore. I was devastated. He told me I couldn't go and see Danny but that if I wanted, I could go and see him at his home. I didn't understand why he couldn't come. He spoilt us so much – we used to have mountains of presents at Christmas and he looked after us. I went to see him at his house. I remember being very shocked. This man that used to buy us everything and he lived in one room – a bedsit. We made cakes and laughed, and he tickled me, and I hugged him, and we sat on the bed and he told me to feel his tummy because it was rumbling so much. I did, then he asked if my tummy was rumbling. He put his hand under my blouse. Felt my tiny nipples but it was OK because that's what Michael Pyre did too, and he wasn't even my daddy. Sean was to me. I never saw Sean again. He never rang me, he moved address. I didn't understand why he had abandoned me until I got older. He was just another one of them, but I guess I had a lucky escape. I was most definitely Sean's favourite and when I look back and think of things I wonder if he ever did abuse me when I was little, but I don't remember. Guess that's one thing I'll never know…

I lived with my nanna, a kind, gentle, beautiful woman but my, did she have a temper! That was normal for me until Sean left. Me, my nanna, my mother and my two sisters Sharon and Melanie. We lived in a huge council estate – not the nicest place to grow up – but my nanna's back garden was my haven. It was beautiful – I used to pretend I was in musicals and sing and dance around the garden. She grew everything, apple trees, pear trees, rhubarb, cherries, tomatoes, lettuce, you name it was in that garden with a beautiful blossom tree right in the middle. Crazy paving all around I used to jump from stone to stone singing my songs, usually Doris Day's Secret Love or something from Seven Brides for Seven Brothers or West Side Story. I loved music – it seemed to take over my whole body. I'd hold on the prop of the washing line and pretend it was my microphone and I was right in the middle of a beautiful Fairy tale. Music has stuck with me my whole life. I connect to every lyric, every melody. It has been the rock that I turn to in times of despair, music has got me through some of the toughest times in my life.

We had a dog called Judy – a whippet. Judy was my best friend – she had the saddest face and the saddest eyes. I'd look into her eyes and talk to her for as long as she could settle next to me. We would sit in the kitchen on the cold tiled floor on a rug which was in the middle and the gas on the cooker to keep us warm. I'd talk to that dog for hours. I have a beautiful memory of my sister Sharon on that rug. I was no more than seven or eight and she was holding me, singing to me, stroking my hair, rocking me. I believe to this day that's the most love I've ever been shown by any of my family. That's one memory I will never let go of. I can't remember what she was singing but I remember that love. I'd never had it, didn't know what it was, what emotion I was going through, but it felt so nice. I've never felt like that since. Sharon had her own room because she was taking exams in school. She was stunningly beautiful and very clever – I recall her leaving school with so many achievements, her room was so pretty she had a white bureau with all her pens and colours laid out immaculately. My nanna was in another room and myself, my sister Melonie and my mum in another – me and Mel in bunk beds, and my mum on a double bed next to us. I was epileptic – don't know when that started, but I know I had my last brain scan and my last Epilim tablet when I was ten. I think my epilepsy was brought on by trauma. I know I used to fit when I couldn't cope with situations – they were more like convulsions. I'd just collapse, faint. I always remember coming to with a cold compress on my head but one thing's for sure – I know the last fit I had and what caused it.

We lived opposite a social club and an adventure playground, spent a lot of time there, the Venny as we called it. Typical council estate park, full of kids that no one really cared about. Kids in their school uniform, who had no dinner and stayed at the park till it shut around nine. Every swear word you've heard bellowing out of the mouths of kids age 5. I used to walk on wooden poles, making dances up with my best friend Paula, to the Pointer Sisters' song, *Frankie*. Me and Paula made dances up to all sorts – I remember the kid's disco in a church and we were dancing to *The Reflex* by Duran Duran. Everyone was in a circle around us whilst we were perfectly synchronised with each other. I've kept in touch with Paula, but only a few hellos on Facebook and some pictures. I've tried to leave everyone behind me from those days. 35 years on she has no clue, but she was a huge part of my life, her and her mother and sister. I spent a lot of time with them, a lot of the time we were getting into bother, but they were my safe place at the time. I have a lot to be grateful to them for. Me and Paula were going clubbing at 11. Drinking bottles of thunderbirds and bottles of 20/20. Her sister was around 15 and we would all go out with her mum. Saturday night in the over 18s and dress down for the Sunday in the same club for kids disco, I remember going out one Saturday and me, Paula and her sister walked straight in and they refused her mum. We were laughing so much, I think her mum must have been too drunk to get in, but we carried on with our night anyway. Most of my childhood memories – the happy ones – are thanks to Paula and I'll never forget her.

I started fitting a lot. I had a rubber Rupert the Bear that I couldn't let go of. He was in pieces from where I used to bite him. Some kids have security blankets – I had rubber Rupert and I couldn't sleep without him. This particular night I remember my nan coming into our bedroom and she was standing at the window huffing and puffing, her slippers on and her grey hair in a hair net – she always put her hairnet on for bed. My sister asked if she was OK and the fiery temper flew out of her – she was a woman possessed, cursing about our mum. "I'm going to go round there and drag her back by the scruff of her hair," she said. "Who are you on about, Nanna?" we asked. "Your bloody mother, in the street making a fool of herself." We looked out of the window and between the houses was a gap and a streetlight – underneath the streetlight was mum with this scruffy-looking man, small, long hair. They were kissing. I remember it upset me so much I started fitting. Sean was my dad and he'd not been here for two weeks and he hurt me. I had never seen my mum even holding hands with Sean but here they were under the streetlight snogging like children. I came to with my nanna's hand on my head with a cold flannel and I'd wet myself. "Come on sweetheart, I'm going to sort this," she said. She went and got Sharon from her room and asked her to look after me and Mel and she marched around the corner. There was no stopping her, we were all peering through the window waiting for her to appear in the gap in the houses. We were giggling because we knew what our nan was like. There she was in the streetlight walking over to Mum and this stranger. She grabbed Mum by the hair and dragged her home kicking and screaming. We all jumped in bed and pretended to be asleep. Our mother was so prim and proper, well known, well liked. I remember her running upstairs once and smacking Mel what seemed so hard because she called me a retard. You couldn't say bloody or fart – they were not allowed to be spoken in our house, but a few weeks later my mum was saying fuck, bastard, and every other word you can think of. We never saw her – she was always out and we didn't know where she was. Nanna was a great support – she used to tell us stories and laugh with us. She was the greatest woman to ever be in my life, strong independent, funny, my hero.

I had to sleep with Mel that night because I'd wet the bed and my nanna came in and took the mattress downstairs. There was no heating in those days – you had the coal fire and the gas rings off the cooker. Next day when I went to primary school, I got called into the headmistress' office –

my mum was there. The house was on fire, she had put the mattress in front of the fire to dry and it fell over and set alight. We were very lucky – it was only downstairs that was destroyed with only one room having smoke damage upstairs. She was all sweetness and light in the office – just warning us and comforting us that everything was OK. As soon as we left the school grounds, she started swearing, going crazy. "You've got to stop wetting the bed, stupid bitch, you're 8 now." I was petrified I'd never seen my mum like this – she was so angry with this hatred in her face I'd never seen. I explained to her that I'd had a fit when she was out the night before and I couldn't help it but she wouldn't leave it alone. It was a two-mile walk to our house from the school and all the way back she just went on and on. From that day, everything went from bad to worse.

Mum introduced us to the scruffy man – Craig. I thought he was a little bit older than Sharon. Me and my sisters used to talk about him – we didn't like him but he had two sisters the same age as myself and Mel called Jane and Susan, and he had a handicapped brother called Ben. They had moved in at the back of us a few months before and my mum was helping them decorate and get settled in. Obviously, now I know that's why Sean couldn't see us anymore, this was Mum's new boyfriend. And that's why we hadn't seen Mum! I spent a lot of time with Jane and Susan. It was good to have friends to play with – I showed them the garden and we would all play nicely together, sometimes it would just be me and Jane and we would put one roller skate on each and go as fast as we could. I fell one day into a barbed wire fence and cut my knee open. Mum was at Craig's, so Susan ran round and Craig came running, picked me up and took me to the hospital to have stitches. A scar I still have to this day. The only physical scar I have that reminds me of him. He was nice to me and we started spending a lot of time together. I think because I was the youngest, I was the easiest to get to come around. The fact that my Mum was with a teenager and she was in her thirties didn't matter to me. I was a child. He would pick me up from school, take me to football matches, buy me ice creams – only me though, not Sharon or Mel.

Something very strange happened from that point on – I don't remember anything about my nanna or my sisters until I got to 10 or 11 – apart from that one memory of Sharon singing to me on the rug in the kitchen. It's like there was no one there but me, not one thing, no matter how hard I try to think about them – I have no memories. It was like they didn't live with me, my world turned into Mum and Craig.

I had a sleepover with Susan and Jane at Craig's. My mum was in the kitchen with him and Craig's mum and dad – all playing Frustration. We were in the bedroom playing with dolls – Mum came up to give me a kiss and said she was going home. We had our nighties on – then Craig came in and told me I needed a bath. He used to tickle me but it hurt, really dig his fingers in and I'd tell him to stop but he always carried on. I got into the bath with my dolly and Craig washed my hair, head tipped back, pouring water over my face with a measuring jug, as he brushed away the hair from my face, his hand stroking my hair right down my back. He would tell me what a good girl I was and would ask me what I wanted to do that week, where I wanted to go. He told me to stand up so he could wash me properly. He started at the top, rubbing the soap in between his palms really fast then rubbing my arms and my tummy, then he would tell me to open my legs so he could do them properly, as he would go up and down rubbing my legs with the soap. When he got to the top, he would move his fingers over and stroke my vagina, then the other leg and the same thing, always still talking about how he was going to treat me and what a good girl I was. Then his finger was inside me. He needn't have bothered really promising me things – I'd already had this done before with Michael Pyre and then touched by

Sean. This was what all grown-ups did to their kids. It was normal.

The following morning, I got up as if nothing had happened. I was told it was our secret and that if I didn't say anything, I would be rewarded. I knew that was true because when I was getting fingered in the back of the car I was dressed as a princess, and Sean bought me presents and took me horse riding so what was different. I went downstairs into the kitchen and Craig was sat at the kitchen table – "Good morning, Princess," he said. I knew it, I was going to be important again!!! I ran over and threw my arms around him. He said he was going to take me for a walk, so I quickly ran upstairs and got dressed. He surprised me with us going to a football match – I was football mad, still am to this day. We went to watch Crewe Alexander – it was around a five-mile walk there and back through fields and there was a little stream you had to jump across, I didn't think I could jump it. I remember standing on the edge, frightened I wouldn't make it, but I did, and Craig spun me round and I was so proud of myself. He constantly praised me for whatever I was doing – how I looked, what I was wearing, how clever I was. I was a very confident child back then – not a care in the world. I was happy and beautiful – everyone told me I was beautiful, especially Craig. It wasn't long before I believed Craig was nicer than Sean – the man I'd known from birth but at that age, you adjust and forget about things and people seem less important as time goes on.

I only wish that was the case with Craig – 40 years on I can still see his face as clear as daylight. We were inseparable. He would pick me up from school, take me for walks and go to the park. He would sit on the back doorstep of my nan's house and watch me skipping or play ball with me, slipping his fingers in my vagina at any given opportunity. It was Craig that bought me my roller skates and he was heartbroken when I fell into the barbed wire – so much so that when he took me to the hospital to get stitches he reminded me not to tell any of the nurses about how special I was to him because they would want to be special too and he would have to stop taking me out and wouldn't be able to spend any more time with me. I didn't want that – I was getting spoiled – my mum was happy – I'd never seen her smiling as much.

What would happen if I told anyone and Craig couldn't give me the attention I wanted and what if my mum stop smiling and being the happy person, she had become. That would all be my fault so why would I say anything. Why would I ruin everything for everyone? I couldn't do that, not now, my mum was so hurt by my biological dad leaving that we weren't allowed to talk to him or talk about him or even see what he looked like because of her cutting him out of every photo, every memory she had. I never even knew of his existence, so I had to make sure my mum was happy too. I had to keep this secret in order for everyone around me to carry on as normal. I was happy – I was loving all the attention I got, and I didn't want anything to change.

Craig had children of his own and an ex-wife, but he never saw any of them – no contact at all. I remember an argument between my mum and Craig and Craig told me he wasn't allowed to see his children because my mum wouldn't allow it and that's why I was so special to him. But now I don't believe that – I believe he was not allowed to see his children because he was and is a paedophile, but I'll never know what happened there. Never say never, I guess! I found stuff out later on in life about Craig so who knows if it happened with his own children and who knows if they would be strong enough to come forward, it's taken me this long to admit the real truth. I have covered for people for years for my own reasons which I'll get to later. I know there are more children than me and he was sick enough to touch his own children. Absolutely!!

As I came towards the end of primary school and was heading into junior school, I was being abused four or five times a week. Craig told me when I got to middle school, things would change because I was becoming a woman. Yes, nine or ten years old and I was a grown-up. Middle school was a very confusing time for me. I fancied my PE teacher and had sexual thoughts about him all the time. Sometimes he would take assembly. He used to make everyone laugh and he let us sing some songs that junior schools had never heard of back then. He was young and trendy and whilst our neighbouring schools were singing hymns, we were singing about bananas. He was a great teacher and my first crush, I wanted to be the best in the class – I wanted him to notice me. I threw myself into netball wing attack! I wanted to be goal attack but was too small. He would call to me, "Good job, Emma," and I used to go all fuzzy inside. We would sit for our break all hot and sweaty after running around for a while and I'd imagine him touching me like Craig did. Mr Reed we called him, but his name was Stephen. He was older than Craig, I think, in his 20s – he was beautiful. I'd get ready for school in the morning, walk those two miles with a smile on my face, knowing I was going to get to see him. I asked Craig one day when I was walking home from school if Mr Reed's daughter, if he had one or when he had one, would do with him what Craig was doing to me. He told me if she was special – only special girls got what he did. I was jealous of his child if he had one. How lucky she would be to have the most beautiful person I'd ever seen, and I had scruffy Craig with his long curly hair, and his worn and tired clothes. He was only around 5ft 4, maybe smaller and he bit his nails and walked like he had a carpet under each arm. And here was Mr Reed – tall, dark, handsome. I was having sexual fantasies in junior school. I was becoming a woman – that's what Craig told me anyway and I believed him.

World Book Day was approaching, and I wanted to look the best, I had to stand out, I had to be noticed by Mr Reed. He would see what effort I'd made and would come and talk to me. Me and my mum decided on Pierre the clown – you know the one with the white face and the lonely tear, I think that is when I found my mask it was the perfect thing for me. I was someone else, I could be whoever I wanted to be for one whole day. No one knew it was me, all in white with a black frilly collar, white face, black eyes with one red tear coming down my face. I remember looking in the mirror and feeling different. I could portray someone else so well, I was back in my garden in a musical. I felt tall and was overwhelmed with happiness – how this mask could make me be whoever I wanted to be. I walked into school proud as punch looking around for Mr Reed. He saw me. "WOW, look at you," he said, "you look amazing!" Job done – he was going to be attracted to me now like every other grown-up was. He was going to touch me and make me feel so much more than Craig, but he walked away. The time came for us to walk around the hall parading our costumes, all in a solid rectangle, one walking behind the other. I was as sad as the tear that was drawn on my face – why did he not want me? I was special – everyone told me so. Then I had a thought – he must have a little girl, he hasn't got room for me because everyone has their own secrets they keep. If he didn't want me, he must have a little girl at home. That made sense to me – that was how I dealt with it. I did look the best – I was going to win this competition and Craig would reward me because Mr Reed couldn't – he had his own little girl. I felt better, I knew I was going to be special in Craig's eyes because he would notice me, he always did. They announced the winner – it was me – I won everything, best dressed on Book Day, best princess in the competition. No wonder Craig and Michael Pyre wanted me. I went up to collect my trophy and got a hug of Mr Reed. I was complete.

PE was different after that – I used to be the one in the school hall getting changed in front of everyone, as we all did, but I'd keep my top off longer, walk around in my knickers hoping to catch his attention. I never did – I didn't even have any breasts, but I caught someone else's eye.

Jake was in my year – he lived around the corner from the school. We would play kiss-chase and American bulldog and it would always be him chasing me. Other people my age were just like me – I would never think of Jake touching me. Why would I? He was like me – little! He asked me if he could be my boyfriend, as children do. I agreed, and we walked around the school playground holding hands. It's only because I won World Book Day I thought to myself. Craig came to pick me up from school – I couldn't wait to tell him I had a boyfriend. He went crazy, told me I wasn't allowed a boyfriend, or he would have to stop being nice to me. WHY? Most kids had boyfriends – some girls had three or four. It didn't matter back then. Will you go out with me? That's what we would say to each other. I told Craig I wouldn't be Jake's girlfriend and he said, that's a good girl.

The next day in school I continued holding Jake's hand and letting him chase me when we played games at break time. He asked me if I wanted to go for tea at his house. I said I'd ask my parents, I couldn't ask Craig, so I asked my mum if I could go for tea at Paula's and said they would drop me back at home. She agreed. We carried on again, holding hands, people telling me, "Ner ner ner ner ner you got a boyfriend" – my little crooked smile beaming. I went for tea – we had some sort of casserole. Then we went into the dining room – I remember they had a piano in there, we were messing about on the piano then decided to have a game of Connect Four. We were sat opposite each other dropping tokens into the frame and it just rolled out of my mouth – "Do you want to play with me?" "What do you want to play?" he said. "Doctors and nurses," I replied. "OK – what do we do?" he said. I got his hand and put it inside my knickers but he ran off crying. Then his mum came in and said it was time to go home, all the way home I was thinking what did I do to make him cry. What have I said – I was only trying to make him feel special? I'll tell him in school tomorrow, I thought, tell him he's special and he will understand then.

Jake never really spoke to me after that and as we grew up, it got worse. I haven't seen him since I moved schools when we reached high school but if I did, what would I say? Would he remember? What did he think of me? Probably the same as everyone else did whilst I was growing up, but looking back I deserved everything they thought. I was everything they said but did I deserve to have the titles I did? Did I deserve the name-calling? Was it my fault? I don't know, I struggle with blame every day. Is it my fault the way I was? The person I wanted to be? It wasn't by choice – it was by need. All I know is, back then I needed it – what it turned me into as an adult is a different story.

Towards the end of junior school, I was a woman. I was shaving my legs and armpits – Craig showed me how the first time. I cut my legs so bad there was blood everywhere. He dried me off and rubbed some cream on my legs – there was blood all over the towel. "We will have to throw this away," he said, "in case your mum sees it – she won't want you growing up. She will get jealous of you." Jealous of me? The woman didn't even speak to me, she hated me. I started hating my mum – I was going to be better than her, I was going to be the special one in Craig's life. Then she could hate me for an actual reason instead of for just being born.

Craig's sisters Jane and Susan became a huge part of my life, but could I look them in the eye today? I don't think so. They were the second stage of my fucked-up life – the new family – as it were. The family of sexually abused fuck-ups that only knew one thing – how to touch. The only emotion we felt was sexual, they had endured this too before I came on the scene – because they were already good at it. Getting fingered by Jane or Susan made me wet – we would kiss for hours, locked in our bedroom, taking it in turns to finger each other or go down and lick each other. Then join in together – every day this happened. We needed it. I never told Craig about me and his sisters – he would have told me to stop like he did with Jake and I didn't want to stop. When Craig wasn't touching me, Jane or Susan was. I wasn't interested in dolls or games or playing out – well, games that led to sex were OK.

When my nan got moved downstairs, I was about nine. She couldn't make it up the stairs for one reason or another. She had a bed in the living room. Me and Susan and Jane turned her bedroom into a sex den. One would wait in my bedroom and the other would be with me in our den having sex together – passionate sex. We would turn it into games – either we were Mummy and Daddy going to bed after a long day, or we would pretend to have a shop but only one person could come in at any one time. But this game was early on in our relationship, when I was sleeping with both of them, but they didn't know. It soon came out and we just had sex together. I never saw my mum – don't know where she was – but she wasn't interested anyway. She could have walked into my room and seen me at eight years old licking another child's vagina and told me it was wrong, but she never came upstairs. If it was bedtime, she would shout up – Emma bed! Never – come down and give me a kiss – just get to bed. In fact, the only time I'd spend with my mum is when we were faking being a happy family at Morris Dancing or beauty competitions or when she wanted one of us to brush her hair for hours. We would sit and brush and brush her hair until our arms ached. Carry on – she would scream. Bitch!!!

I think about Jane and Susan a lot. I know I wasn't the only one, which makes me wonder about his own family. I wonder how his kids turned out, I wonder if they are OK or if they are like him? I wonder if Jane and Susan think about the times we shared together. I wonder if it has made them like me. I wonder if they have grown up feeling like a paedophile and a predator like I have. I wonder if they despise themselves and can't accept anyone caring about them. So many wonders and never any answers. I lost my own head hiding things away, I lost all sense of respect for who I was, and it made me very poorly. Mentally and physically to a point where I wanted to give up – surrender myself to the devil because that's where I am going. The level of sexual abuse that has surrounded my life and destroyed every relationship I've ever had, every choice I've ever made. Some people say you have to move forward and forget the past – it's the person you are that defines you. What if you don't like the person you are? How do you get past that? How do you become someone you want to live with every day, when you eat yourself alive, when you can't look at yourself in the mirror without having flashbacks of how evil you were, when you want to pretend it was all a dream but it wasn't?

Walk a day in my shoes, have one day in my head and then tell me the past doesn't define you. The past shapes you and it has shaped me into a loveless cold-hearted stone that won't let anyone in, that thinks people want something if they're nice to you, that doubts everything she does, that doesn't see the good in herself. A shell with no self-confidence that puts this mask on every day – a mask that's a fun-loving, crazy, feisty woman that attracts people but then when I start to feel vulnerable and wanted and the soft side of me – the real me – tries to make an appearance, they walk all over me or push me to the side and don't want me anymore. Every rejection has helped build my fort, every face has helped bury my soul.

All I want is to be loved, but how can you love someone that doesn't know how to take it or believe it or show any emotion? Am I the only one that feels like this – does Jane or Susan? Do they torture their own lives or are they strong enough to bury the past? I buried it for 45 years. I caved because I gave my heart to someone who I believed in. I have struggled since our breakup to let go. I have struggled letting go of the one thing I believed was true, but it wasn't real, but I couldn't accept it. I still saw him because he told me he would always care about me. When he did see me, he wanted me to stay with him, so I thought he would want me back but even after meeting up for drinks after we split up, then spending the night with him, still making love, he didn't want me. I stayed at his house a whole weekend, went to a wedding with him, slept in the same bed, went to London the next day, came back and slept in the same bed but he didn't want me. It tortured my head and my heart. There have not been many people I have let in, not many I have trusted. I've just gone along with it, even telling people I loved them when I don't really know what it meant or how it feels to receive or give love. I'd changed the person I was, so going back and sleeping with someone who wasn't going to love me or want me in his life anymore was a bad move. Sleeping in the same bed as someone who once held you and said they loved you – why would I do that to myself? I did, but I won't again. He set me back so far, he put my walls so high I couldn't touch them, and I feel sorry for anyone who wants to try and get close to me again.

I have always been a doubter, always been afraid but now I don't think I will ever believe anyone again. Does that make me feel alone? Yes, of course, but who could put up with my battles, who could put up with how fragile I am? Especially when I can't talk, it's now six months since we split, six months since I had my breakdown and I'm still hurting so much. I just want my life back. In four weeks' time, it will be a year since I first met this man who turned my world around. I have tried telling him to stay away from me, but I can't, I have tried shouting at him, but it doesn't help, but as I sit here today pouring out my feelings and heart, I smile to myself. I loved. I actually fell in love – I felt it. I felt the desire to be with someone. I felt the passion of wanting to make someone happy. I wanted to please him, wanted to spend the rest of my days with him. I guess I should put that down as my first milestone. I've achieved something. As I write my story over time, I'm grateful for things. And as much as I will never forget him, he made me feel things I'd never experienced but do I want to continue holding on for something I can't have? I can't do that anymore – my story has started with him and will hopefully end with me feeling OK about us. Who knows what will happen when I get to the end of this who knows where I will be?

I am dating someone at the moment. Do I trust him? No. Do I think he can understand my moods and emotional state of mind? No. Do I think sex is an important factor in his life – Yes! I want to be made love to – for someone to really want me. I went through an emotional rollercoaster regarding sex – thinking naughty sex would make me feel OK. Doing anything I hadn't done as a child. That way I wouldn't think about it, but I long for someone to take those feelings and make me feel so loved that it's OK to look at me and make me feel that making love is a beautiful thing. Maybe I just want someone who doesn't like sex at all, or maybe I am just being me as per usual and am completely unable to decide about what I want. Who I want and what I'm doing next?

My relationship with Jane and Susan continued, but we took it to another level. We started hanging around with a girl who lived a few doors up. I remember thinking she was very stern and a bully when I first met her, but she was actually OK. She had a huge willow tree in her front garden. It was enormous, almost taking over the whole garden. I loved playing under that tree – another bit of nature that I felt at peace with. The willows went all the way to the floor, we could hide behind them. It wasn't too long before we were letting her join in our games. She was part of the sex club, she was part of more guilt and anger in my head. She was another one I took advantage of. Her house was set back off the main road, a huge front garden with this enormous tree looking so beautiful. But inside the house was another story. It was so messy, but messy was good for us – there were so many places to hide. I don't really remember seeing her parents – a vague picture of her mum, but I think she was like me. She was allowed to do whatever she wanted, but saying that, we were at her house quite a bit, so maybe her mum actually cared where she was. Mine wouldn't have noticed if I was there or not by this point. She was too wrapped up in the boyfriend that played with me probably more than her.

I look at my granddaughter now who's ten, beautiful and innocent as a child should be. Ten was a horrible age for me, but I have to go back a few years before I can go forward. I have to write about painful things that I have been trying to hold back from writing. Things I never wanted to disclose, things I never thought I would ever tell another living soul. The things that came flooding back when I had my breakdown. The things I'd locked up for so long. It was these things that made me start my writing and this writing is what's giving me the strength to carry on the past few months. This writing has been my release and I have to talk about everything in my younger life and adult life. I can't hold back, I have to be true to myself, to get out of me every bit of pain I've suffered and until I've done that, I'm not going to be able to heal. So, I need to let go of my feelings towards the birth canal, the holding bay, the one person who could have changed my life but she just made it worse, the disgrace of a woman who had the title mother!!!

I have set myself a goal – I am going to France in three weeks' time and I know there I will find peace in the open country air. I am going to take myself off on a beautiful walk armed with my laptop and release the demons in a safe environment where no one can hurt me or judge me or even know me. That is where she will be revealed. That is where I'll let go.

I am currently sat in the hospital – I have lost count of the number of hospitals visits I have had over the last few months, in fact over the years. It is like my second home. I had a tumour removed from my rectum five weeks ago and as I sit here by myself waiting for yet another scan I find myself reflecting over what might be. I think of all the times (even though I'm not religious) I have found myself reaching out to God or to the people that have passed whom I have cared for. I remember all the times I have begged them to take me to them. I've asked so many times for it to be my turn, so many times for them to see my pain and let me give up. So, as I sit here today what am I hoping for? Today it's – let it be my time – I've had enough. Tomorrow who knows, but today it's my time. I'm watching people walking past me wondering what their troubles are, wondering if they can see mine by my teary eyes. Today I'm weak and it's not with worry, it's with the sheer tiredness I feel for surviving. I don't want to be the woman who is strong, as people keep reminding me because they are not seeing the real me. They are not seeing me sat here in the hospital waiting and hoping it's my time, hoping I can go find my nanna and for her to hold me and tell me everything's going to be OK. I feel so vulnerable sat here, a woman who's almost 46 and sitting here like a child willing to die. A busy hospital but with a calming feeling – illness, death – everything happens here. I'm sat here thinking about the mortuary – lying there all peaceful. I know they are irrational thoughts if said out loud, but they're my thoughts. I could be happy here. I need to learn a lot more about depression and PTSD. It's OK being on pills to try and make you forget these feelings, but they don't, they just numb them. I thought my diagnosis was a cover-up for me being fucked in the head, for me not understanding my own thoughts but they're real and no number of tablets is going to take them away from me. They're all I have left, I can't let go of them, I'm too badly scarred. I think the worst of every situation, I think the worst of every person.

I have tried to reach out to people in the past but because I'm so damn good at playing the clown, I'm so good at hiding things, I honestly think they believe I'm OK – just having a bad day. Again, that's my fault. I blame myself for everything but don't show it. Looking in, I guess you would think I was a selfish person but I'm not. I just can't describe how I feel or let go of the guilt. I continue to live my life in self-destruct mode. I try to pretend things aren't happening around me and the way I deal with that is either alcohol or locking myself away in my room every chance I have. I'll either finish work and stay and drink or go home and hide in bed. There is no in-between with me – I have no balance. I've lost all my friends since my breakdown. I don't see them anymore. I don't see anyone. I know that's my fault. If something is going wrong or I feel pressure, I just run away. I don't mean to – I've done it with friends, relationships. I just run, I have lost some amazing friends because of it. I wish I could have been more supportive when they needed me but instead, I just threw myself into work hiding behind my four walls. If I didn't have Dave and Brenda, God knows where I would have been right now!!! Six feet under no doubt.

2:

The Rise of The Slut

We moved out of Nan's house when I was 10 and into our first family unit with Craig. Another council house, but in a better area than Nan's. It was quiet – twelve houses, six on one side and six on the other with a walkway and some grass in between. The kind of place where you didn't really speak to the neighbours. Everyone kept themselves to themselves, just the occasional hello if you passed in the street – that would be it. Our house had a garage at the back and that was how we used to access the house through the back way. We never used the front door, so it was very rare for us to see anyone. That kind of makes sense to me now, I don't think they wanted us to be friendly with anyone. Didn't want anyone knowing our business. Our house was the end semi – the kitchen was small, with a shed in the middle of it which stored the chest freezer and mother's cigarettes. There was a downstairs toilet and a dining room which was where we spent all of our time. We had a living room, but we weren't allowed in there. That was where visitors were allowed when they came, which wasn't very often. It was always immaculate, pristine, every cushion at a perfect angle – no clutter. When you did sit in there, it was uncomfortable – cold and uninviting. My mum collected red glass. She had clowns and vases – lots of pieces in immaculate condition but they were on top of her wardrobe. You couldn't touch it or see it. Why have nice things and hide them away?

We were allowed to sit in the back room, the one people didn't see, the room that smelt of cigarettes. My mother was a heavy smoker – Peter Stuyvesant was her brand of choice. You would always see a cigarette in her hand or hanging out of her mouth. Even over the cooker, making tea, coughing her smoker's cough over the food. I know I was little, but my mother always looked really old, even in her thirties as she must have been then. She looked so much older. Upstairs – where I spent most of my time – the first room was my sisters', Sharon and Mel. They shared a room with the bathroom next door. There was a small box room which belonged to me and then my mother's and Craig's room. I spent most of my time outside my room in a small hallway with my Sindy dolls and house. I could play for hours with my dolls, they used to sleep with each other and touch each other. Imagine sat on the floor, tapping your dolls around, pretending they're walking and talking and kissing each other, then having to lie on my mother's bed and think about what I was going to do next with Sindy whilst Craig was pushing his penis inside me, then just getting up with cum dribbling down my legs and going back to playing with the dolls as if nothing had happened. That was my life.

Most kids play shop or families with their dolls when they're little. Some pretend their dolls have husbands or boyfriends but that's normal – we grow up with a Dad or a Mum's boyfriend or Dad's girlfriend, so pretending you have a boyfriend is natural because it's what you know. All my time with my dolls was to do with sex. They would get undressed, kiss and go down on each other. I remember asking Craig what was wrong with my male dolly – he didn't have a dick!! Craig told me he couldn't have one because he wasn't old enough, he was only a baby, he wasn't a grown-up like him or me. Does that make me a baby playing with dolls I asked him, but he thought it was a good idea I could teach them what happened when they got a little older. I just think he wanted me away from my sisters. I don't remember them being there anyway. I guess I spent a lot of time on my own with my dolls or in my room or my mother's room. Craig was very secretive. He had a briefcase which was locked every time he went upstairs. He would lock the door, never keep it open and I never knew what was in that briefcase. Maybe it was sex toys, maybe it was porn or maybe it was just full of his secrets that we weren't allowed to know about. Whatever it was, I don't think my mum knew about it because he would always lock himself in the room on his own.

I also don't remember what happened to Judy our beautiful dog. Did they give her up when they got their own place? She couldn't have stayed with Nan, she couldn't even look after herself. Still makes me angry that we left Nan – she needed looking after, she was so old and frail. My mother used to go and see her every day but that soon stopped – she had to be there for Craig. Not for us, but she waited on him hand and foot. Unless she was making stew or a Sunday roast, I would have an 18p margarita pizza to come home to every night – the ones that are cheap brands – I think it was my Mum's own which was a famous brand back then. She would make Craig a hot meal when he got in from work, mine took 25 seconds in the microwave.

Our first animal in this house was a big fat ginger cat called Tabby. We used to say, "The cat's home," and laugh that the house used to shake as he walked down the path. I'm guessing he was male with a name like Tabby. Once again, I formed a bond with the cat, talking to him every night when I was falling asleep. When we first used to live in the house, I shared a room with Mel but when Sharon left, I went into the little box room. I liked that room – it came in useful as I got older because it had a lock on the door. We had blow air heating in the house and I'd sit on top of it until I couldn't breathe because as soon as you moved within five minutes you would be freezing cold. My mother used to shout at me – move out the bloody way, it's freezing. So, I'd just go upstairs and play with my dolls, out the way. I like my own company probably because I spent so much time on my own when I was little. My mother and Craig were at work, I didn't see my sisters and it would just be me and Tabby and my microwave pizza, but I liked it that way. I wasn't feeling the prickles of Craig's pubic hair or the pain of his penis inside me. Obviously, I didn't have any pubic hair – I was a child. I hated that feeling like wire on my smooth vagina. I didn't know what it was until I got older. Now I hate it, that feeling always reminds me of him, which isn't a good feeling when you're fucking someone else.

When I started High school, I was 11. I remember my first day – burgundy skirt, pink and white check blouse with a huge collar – I mean I could have taken off, if a gust of wind had got behind me it was that big, it went past my shoulders! A burgundy jumper and socks that came just under the knee and black patent shoes. Of course, my uniform was always perfectly clean and ironed, my mother had to show she was taking care of me. I couldn't be dirty, I got sent home once in primary school when the nit nurse used to come around. My mother was furious especially as every Sunday night was bath night in our house. So, after my finger off Craig, she would religiously do our hair with Periderma nit lotion which was more like a paste. She would sit and rub it into every bit of our scalp until our heads were red raw, even though we didn't even have nits. So, you can imagine her face, when one of her perfect little kids got sent home with nits. She made me sit on the floor and she examined every little bit of my head every strand of my hair. I was a skinny child with buck teeth – I'd fallen over the handles of a bike when I was around eight and smacked my mouth on the handlebars. I had long mousy brown hair which went past my bottom, it felt like I was sat on that floor forever – it was a good few hours. "Right, get your coat on," she said, and she marched me up to the clinic. "I want to see the woman that told my child she had nits this morning," she said very politely. We went into a room and my mum made her go through every bit of my head. "Dandruff," Mum said, "she has a bit of dandruff." The nit nurse agreed and apologised to my mother who went on to tell her our regimental routine every Sunday night and how far she took it for us not to get nits. Dandruff or not, as soon as we got home, "Sit down," she said again, and I had to go through it all again, but this time I had to sleep with it on my hair. It smelt so bad – then up at the crack of dawn to wash it out and go through it with the nit comb one more time. I think she must have thought she was playing with a doll's head – the ones that were just a head and shoulders and you could put makeup on and fix their hair – because she pulled every strand of hair. My head would go backwards and forwards and then when she had finished she would put my long hair up in a bobble and my head was that sore, I couldn't touch it.

My first day of High School was a challenge, the first was being in the same class as Jake. He wouldn't even look at me – it was the first time a boy or man had made me feel unimportant and I couldn't grasp it. What was wrong with me? Why didn't he want to touch me? He wasn't the last person to make me feel ugly, but he was the first. I didn't find the good kids interesting. Here was me on free school meals because my "family" were in the poor category, so I had a lunch pass. My first day I was stood there not really knowing what was going on. I'd always just got a meal and milk when I was younger, but now I was in a queue with other disadvantaged kids. The poor kids in one queue outside come rain or shine and the kids whose parents could afford to pay for lunch on the other side, that was society! That's where you made a choice – you were either stuck in the poor queue or laughing like the rich kids, it was an embarrassment. The school put you into categories, which was wrong. It shouldn't have been like that. You didn't feel cool and back then, on my first day of daunting high school I wanted to fit in – I wanted to be cool. I wasn't confident anymore. I was a small fish in a big sea and there were some frightening kids, but I worked them out straight away – the ones that everyone was frightened of – the bullies, the ones that could be bullied, the ones that didn't care – all they wanted was an education. Now I know those kids were the ones that were loved. They were confident – they didn't care if they had to fit in or not, didn't care that they had to be liked. They were the kids that went home every night and their parents asked them how their day was, they were the kids that sat down and talked over dinner when they got home, instead of having a 25-second, cheap microwave pizza.

I couldn't be like them – I didn't care if I didn't get an education. What was more important to me then was fitting in, but even more important than that was wanting boys to notice me. I noticed them – I thought about them touching me. When I was in a lesson, I'd go around the room thinking what each person would want to do to me and how they would satisfy me. I'd think about their penis, then remember what Craig told me about them not being grown up. I'd think about them all, except Jake. He didn't want me. Bad mistake, Jake, if you didn't want me someone else will. I was getting sex at home like all the other kids were – that's what I thought, but in school, I had to be wanted, I had to be pretty, I had to be everything everyone had ever shown me I was. But I wasn't, and I didn't know how to handle that. Then it came to me. I know how I could make them feel good and then they would know how special I was, I'd suck their dick, I'd swallow their cum. That's when I became the person I hate now – that's when the rise of the slut began.

I went home from school after my first day, I had been put in the bottom set for most things. I liked that I was with all the kids that wanted a laugh, I was with the ones that made fun of the teachers. Sometimes I would cringe about the stuff that happened when teachers walked out, crying, because of the abuse they got. Mr Rudge, he spoke through his nose so straight away that was something for the class to pick up on, every opportunity someone would take the piss. They would make paper planes and throw them at him, mimic him when he spoke, until one day he walked out. He had had enough – he was in tears and we all laughed. He never returned to school, I wonder if he had a breakdown. I know now he is one of the many people I think about when I'm reflecting on my younger years, I hope he ended up OK.

I walked down the path of our house to be greeted by Tabby. He was sat on a bunker outside where we stored the rubbish bin. I couldn't wait to get in and tell my mother and Craig about my first day in big school. I stroked Tabby for a few minutes and spoke to him about my day then went to open the door. It was locked, I knew the drill well by then, so I tipped the rubbish bin up picked up the key which was stored underneath and let myself in. Just me then, I thought. Went in, put my pizza in the microwave, got a plate, put a huge dollop of red sauce on the side. By the time I had done that, my dinner was ready. I sat at the dining room table, ate my food, then went upstairs and hung my uniform up otherwise Mum would go mad. I put on my clothes – back then it was leggings and a t-shirt usually matching. I had blue leggings and a blue t-shirt, white, red, and yellow all matching. I must have looked like a giant banana when I wore the yellow ones. I always had my hair up and I loved to get dirty – I think that's because I always had to be so pretty. I think that's when I started rebelling, when I walked in from big school and had no one to talk to about it when I got home. I knew my mother didn't like me, anyway, so where could I go from here? I had to fit in with the bullies, I had to befriend them and be accepted, I had to pull out my mask and make them see how funny I was, how dangerous I could be, how rebellious I was towards my family. If I could prove that, they would like me.

Craig came home from work. He told me, first, that we didn't have long and to get upstairs, open my legs wide and shout for him – telling him I needed him. I went upstairs, took off my leggings and t-shirt and shouted as he had demanded – "Craig, come upstairs, I need you." "Not good enough," was what I got back. "Craig, come upstairs we haven't got long," again in a nasty tone of voice, "tell me to come upstairs and eat your sweet vagina, that's all I've needed all day, make it work," he said, "or you will be in trouble." So, I said it, I didn't want to be in trouble. He walked in the room and stood there and just stared at me legs spread. "Touch yourself," he said. I didn't understand. "Touch where?" I asked. "Put your finger inside like I do, and tell me you're a dirty bitch." I did as he asked, he came to the side of the bed and wanked over me, cumming on my diddies as everyone called them. They weren't breasts – I wasn't developed – they were diddies.

"Now go wipe yourself up before your mum gets back." I was sat in the bathroom not thinking about what had just happened, but I was really upset, I started to cry. He didn't even ask how my first day at big school went.

The following day I came up with an action plan, I was going to win these people over by being naughty and funny and they would let me join the cool gang. I went downstairs – obviously no one was there, so I made myself some sugar puffs, went into the garage, carefully opened a packet of mother's cigarettes. I would open the thin clear cellophane that wrapped around them, then open the gold paper that protected the cigarettes ever so carefully, take a few cigarettes out from the back, then put the gold paper back on and lick the cellophane until it stuck. Everyone would think I was cool if I smoked, wouldn't they? It can't be that hard, I thought. Mum's always got a fag hanging out of her mouth. I walked the short walk to school and all the cool kids were hanging outside the gym. So, I lit up my first cigarette in clear view of everyone, not just the cool kids. I put it in my mouth then one of them shouted. I lifted my cigarette in the air and shouted back. I got the nod of approval and walked over to them all, absolutely shaking inside, but my mask was protecting me, so I was fine. "What's your name?" said one of the girls, "Emma," I replied. "How long have you smoked for?" "Since I was about nine, I just steal them off my mum, she doesn't notice." "OK," she said, "bring me a full packet tomorrow. We'll sell them, keep some for ourselves and make enough to get some alcohol for a party tomorrow night." "OK, no worries," I said. I was cool, I was one of them and if that meant stealing off my mum so be it, she hated me anyway. I stood there and for one second, I felt big and confident again, I lifted the cigarette to my mouth puffed on it and blew it straight out and started coughing. Everyone started laughing. "You don't even know how to smoke properly," they said. "No, it just went down the wrong hole," – that was an expression I'd picked up from my mum when she started one of her coughing episodes. They all walked off and just left me, stood there on my own. OK, plan B. I needed to learn how to smoke by morning and have some cigarettes then surely, they would let me in.

I woke up in the morning and had a bath. Craig told me I needed to bathe every morning and every night. I went downstairs – just me as always. I prepared my sugar puffs, sat at the table and thought about my action plan. Would Mum notice if I took a whole packet of cigarettes? She hadn't said anything about the few I took from the back of her packet. She hadn't noticed the ripped cellophane or if she had, she just probably thought it was her, the bitch, but wouldn't say anything because of her guilt or maybe she never said anything because I was the same height as her by then and she knew I could go for her.

I believed when I got older that if Craig got sent away, I would have my mum back – the one that was so loving when Sean was in our lives, the one that didn't swear, the mother that wanted us to be beautiful, the mother that made us a meal at dinner time, but looking back how could I have thought that? I wasn't facing one paedophile – I was facing five – in a world of no DNA. I was stuck in a world of your word against mine and here I was, a rebellious shit of a child, protecting my mum and her pathetic boyfriend to make them happy. I still do that to this day – try and please people and make them happy when they don't deserve it. Pretend I'm fine about things and inside I'm crumbling. They made me that way – they taught me that I had to keep my mouth shut and get on in life. They turned me into the slut I became, because I didn't know anything but how to fuck.

When I was getting washed in the bath by Craig when I was 7 or 8, he would take me into his brother's room. There was a kind of bunker in the corner – it was the box room – a square, but I don't know what was underneath. I had to sit on that bunker, whilst he would tell his brother what to do to me. He is a spastic and one thing I know I could never blame him for the years he spent touching me. He would sit downstairs with his mum and dad and clap and rock backwards and forwards. He couldn't grasp normality, he didn't understand it, he didn't know I was a baby, he didn't know that it was wrong, but he liked it. I could tell by his happy clapping. He looked forward to these nights. "Open your legs," Craig would demand, then would tell his brother to finger me, show him how to do it and Ben loved it. That wasn't his fault – it was Craig's – he was teaching someone that didn't know what sex was how to do it on a child. Our nights continued until Craig wanted me to have sex with his brother. We went into the box room – his brother was sat on the bed, rocking and clapping, waiting to touch me. My legs opened – he started putting his fingers inside and laughing – he was excited. I had to wank him until he went hard. His brother didn't know what an erection was and kept looking at his penis and looking at Craig. That's it – Craig would say, as Ben stood there laughing, his head moving from left to right. Craig pushed my legs wide open, he took hold of his brother's dick and pushed him towards me. "Let him in, push forward," he said. I had him inside me for the first time with Craig behind him pushing and pushing him. His brother dribbling and clapping. I started to bleed with the force of Craig's thrusts on his brother. He never cum, so once again I was wanked over. It was over. I got up went into his sisters' room, got in bed with Jane and started to kiss her. I don't know if I was horny – how could I know, I was a baby, but she made me feel OK and I settled.

The threesome between me, Ben and Craig continued. I can still feel the spit from Ben, still see him laughing and clapping when he was fucking me and Craig pushing him into me backwards and forwards. "Good girl," he would say, "doing it right for Daddy." I was good at doing it right for Daddy. He was my Daddy now and I had to do what he wanted. Craig's parents were downstairs watching TV and a threesome going on in the box room. Craig's parents were old, his mum had a hair lip and talked funny to me. His dad didn't do anything, he got waited on hand and foot and would sit in the living room all day in his trousers and vest with braces and his huge belly hanging over. The only thing he would do was make gravy for the Sunday roast. I do the best gravy, he would say, but he mixed lard with not so much stock or granules and the roast was covered in white fat – it was disgusting. Ben must have been in his late twenties or early thirties. He was always in black; tracksuit bottoms and t-shirts.

He loved the music to Coronation Street – you could tell that made him happy when it started. The clapping got faster, as did the rocking. He couldn't speak a word just moans every now and then, but he soon became used to it and when we would walk into the bedroom, he would put his fingers straight out and laugh. It was different – something new – he didn't have a clue what was going on, but I didn't know either. He was touching me with Craig's help – he never would have done it on his own. Craig told him to lick my vagina one night and he went down licked me once and went into a mad rage smacking his head, screaming. Craig was trying to calm him down – he obviously didn't like it. There was no calming him, he was like the devil possessed. I quickly got dressed just in time before his mum walked in. "Sshh, sshh," she said – she just thought he was having a moment, one of his episodes, but it wasn't – it was because of me. I don't know what happened to Ben. When we moved to our new house, I never saw him again. He could never tell anyone what he did – he would never stand up for me. He would just clap, and rock and I would love so much to meet the guy who never knew how much he hurt me. I'd hug him and apologise even though he wouldn't understand. But if I got the chance, he deserves that and I need to tell him it's OK. Poor bastard.

Craig bought me my first computer – it was an Atari and I had a tennis game. It was basically a white block either side and you had to pass it backwards and forwards but it was a computer and I was grateful. I sat in the dining room whilst mum was choking over the Sunday dinner. I was playing on my new game and Craig walked over put his hand up my blouse and was rubbing my diddies round and round. I just carried on playing my tennis. I knew it would stop soon because Mum was there, but it didn't. There he was rubbing my non-existent breasts and Mum was there talking to him. I just sat there listening to the click of each ball as I hit it, back and forth, concentrating on getting the highest score. Craig rubbing my diddies and Mum watching, they were my parents and it was OK. I finished my game, sat down and had dinner, then got sent to my room. I wasn't bothered though, I had to learn how to smoke. I went up to my room knowing that I wasn't going to be bothered by anyone. I opened the window, stuck my head outside, putting the net curtains behind me and started puff by puff – coughing, but eventually, I could do it without coughing. Got into bed and fell asleep. My mum smoked that much even if she did come upstairs, she would not have been able to smell it. But she wouldn't come up anyway, she never did.

I went to school the next day with the fags I'd stolen from Mum. I didn't wear my shirt with the big collars instead I wore a t-shirt. Third day and I was rebelling. I walked past the gym trying to ignore people, pretending I didn't give a shit. "Emma, Emma," they called. I looked over, gave a wave and walked over to them. "You got the cigs?" they said. "Yeah, of course, told you I can take what I want from home." I lit up a cig, inhaled it, blew it out without coughing and no one said a word. "I'll give you 10," I said, "I need 10 or I'll be without a fag." "OK, we will sell 10 for £1 each and have enough money for beer." "Who is going to buy a cig for £1," I said, "when they're only 90p to buy a packet?" "Watch and learn," they said, and it was easy.

At lunchtime we went to the lunch queue, but instead of standing on the poor side, I followed my new friends to the posh side. "Buy my dinner pass," they demanded, "you can get a meal and we need the money." Straightaway they agreed because they were frightened. We all sold our dinner passes for £1 each and made them buy a cigarette for another pound. This was an everyday thing – by the time second break came we had enough money for more fags, some cheap booze and some weed off the ice cream van that used to come to school every day. Imagine the excitement of the ice cream van outside your school every day. It was a great cover-up and we had money now. I didn't have to hand my pass in for lunch anymore. I didn't have to feel like an outcast. I had real money in my hand and although some kids did by ice cream, we clubbed together, got some dope and more cigs and had enough left over for some sweets. We had a business at 11 years old – a real enterprise between us. We were doing OK… and for sure now I was allowed to go to the party they mentioned, and I was going to drink alcohol. I'd never drunk before – I'd had the occasional snowball at Christmas and I recall having a baby sham, but I'd never tasted real alcohol or felt the effects of it – that was phase 2. Learning to drink!

My mum never drank – the occasional shandy now and then, but lucky for me people used to buy her alcohol for Christmas, and she had quite a collection. My mum had two brothers and three sisters with lots of nieces and nephews. There were also some people you had to call auntie, but they weren't really. When mum got with Craig, we never saw anyone from the family except for funerals and my eldest sister's wedding. I'm sure my sisters saw them, but I know I never did.

I went home from school feeling really happy. I'd made friends, made some money and I was going to go to a party, drink alcohol and smoke weed and obviously fuck – that's what everyone did. No one was in so I made my pizza, got a bottle of red wine – it must have taken me half an hour to get the cork out – went upstairs and drank it, not all of it, maybe a glass or two. I was drunk, I was sat on the end of my bed, the room spinning, feeling sick. This wasn't a nice feeling – why does anyone do this? Tabby came into my room and I started crying. "I love you Tabby, you're so beautiful," I said, then laid down my head on the pillow and I was out like a light.

When morning came my head was banging and I rushed to the bathroom and was sick. I tried to get ready for school, but I couldn't move for what seemed forever. I went downstairs – no one there, as usual – so went back upstairs and got into bed. No school for me today I thought and so I slept. I woke up at two in the afternoon, had my bath, got dressed and stood outside the school gates puffing on my cigarette. "Where have you been today?" they asked when they came out. "Felt like shit," I said, "went to a party last night, didn't get in till 8 this morning, couldn't be arsed coming to school." They all started laughing. "Emma, you're mad, love it."

Another lie, the first of many in fact, but I was liked, and I wasn't bullied by anyone. The next few months were easy. I was smoking outside at every break, swearing, making people laugh. It felt great. I was part of the elite club that everyone else hated. We were the naughty kids – the bullies and I was slowly turning into one too. I would go home after school and there was no one home so then go straight out, sometimes not getting in till the early hours of the morning, but the key was always left outside, and I had Tabby to talk or cry to anyway. There were two girls in school that everyone was scared of – two girls that I wanted to be friends with – then no one would hurt me. That's how I saw things, make friends with the hard girls and then no one would touch you.

I hated lessons – I was easily distracted, mainly by looking around for my next fuck. In the first three months of high school, I'd slept with five people. We used to go out at night, hang around the shops, smoke weed, drink thunderbirds and have sex. But that was normal at home, so why should it be any different in school? I think I was good at sex and the boys wanted me. They made me feel OK and I made them feel great. Life was good – we were making money in school, sleeping with lots of people and having a laugh, so why would I want that to change, but it did.

There was a school play and as much as I hated lessons, I loved music and drama so when this production came up, I wanted to be involved. I went into the hall where the auditions were being held, picked up the script and just picked someone out. They don't sound very important, I thought, I'll go for this part (which I thought was a man who didn't say too much). The school was so excited about this production, because it was in the local newspaper and was a part of some music festival for our district. It was going to be recorded, it was to run over five days, there were press and professional pictures that had to be taken, so it was a big thing for our school – half-filled with the council estate kids.

I walked on the stage. "Zip your lip, Wisey, I'm in no mood for conversation," I said. "OK, can you sing *I'm feeling fine?*" they shouted, so I started. The key was way too high for me, but I got through as best I could. "Thank you," they said. We had to wait two days to find out who had been given a part. I sat in the hall that day, hoping I had it with sweaty hands and my heart beating so fast then it started. Bugsy Malone part goes to so and so and Blousey Brown goes to Emma!! I couldn't believe it – I was so excited, but I wasn't just an extra, as I had thought, I was Bugsy's interest – his girlfriend! I had to sing twice on my own and with others, but my singing was so bad in the audition I thought they had made a mistake. Here was me in the first year of high school, getting cast a major part in a play that was going to be spread over five nights, that 1,000 people were coming to watch and I couldn't reach the notes. Why did they pick me?

The next day at break our music teacher came to me and said he needed me to come at lunchtime to practice my songs. Lunchtime was when we all hung out, bullied a few kids and smoked, but I agreed. I walked into the music department and the teacher said, "So obviously you cannot reach the high notes, but you have potential." He made an arrangement which I could cope with and as soon as I started singing, I fell in love with the song, with the emotion and with my character. We had three months to perfect it and that was all I could think about. Suddenly I didn't want to fit in with the cool kids, I wanted to be here in the middle of the drama hall, practising and practising my lines, my songs. I was going to be seen by 200 people a day – I had to get this right. I wasn't smoking or drinking – I was either in the drama hall rehearsing or in my back-garden singing, learning the words over and over whilst trying to perfect my terrible American accent. I started drifting away from the cool kids. I didn't have time to be with them.

There was a girl I met whilst rehearsing – she was in the final year of high school. I'd never seen anyone as beautiful as her and she danced like an angel, a ballerina – I was in awe of her. We became friendly – I think she saw me as a little child that she could look after. If only she had known – I was a grown-up inside that child's body and I'd probably had sex more times than she'd ever had. The time came when the newspaper wanted to take our photos, but it was just of me and Bugsy Malone. We went outside in the school grounds – me in my 1950s dress and hat and for once my long hair flowing and Bugsy in his suit. He has gone on to be quite successful in television. I approached him on Facebook and asked him if he still had the recording of our production, and he did. I sent him a memory stick and he's sent it to me through the post. I've not watched it yet. I'm afraid of seeing the vulnerability in me, afraid to see the child I was. Afraid to look back and see little me. And afraid of hearing me make such a mess of two beautiful songs.

So, the press was there, and they took our photos – they looked like something out of a movie. We looked so good together, we looked in love. I still have those photos – I still have those memories. The first-night performance seemed to come by really quickly – we had foam pies and foam guns just like the film. I was told I wasn't allowed to get hit by a pie because it would ruin my dress and hat. Each night we went out and performed to our best ability and each night just before the last scene of Bugsy Malone where there's a big fight and pies and foam get squirted everywhere, I had to run backstage and watch all the fun enfolding in front of me. On the last night, they told me I was allowed to go on stage – well as soon as I walked out and everyone saw me, I had pies thrown at me, guns splattering foam all over me – it was so funny. I loved every moment of it. When me and Bugsy took the final bow at the end of our five-day project, the whole place went wild. My mum and Craig weren't there, they never came to any of the five nights, they missed me singing and dancing and acting. For me, I class that moment as one of the biggest achievements in my life but also as one of the worst. My world was about to change again. I was about to go from being the bully to the one being bullied.

Everything changed after the play, no one liked me. The boys I'd been having sex with were now slapping me across the hands and head with their rulers. The people I used to get sweets off wouldn't give me any any more. My dinner pass wasn't being bought – I was alone again. Alone at home, alone at school, I had no idea what I'd done wrong. I'd been funny to the girls and got them cigarettes. I'd been complimentary to the boys and let them fuck me. I guess it was because I'd chosen the play over them – they suddenly saw me as some sort of geek, when it was an amazing experience for me. I was friendly with all the older kids in the last year who I'd performed with, but the people I needed – the ones in my year – they hated me. I needed a phase three and when I got there, it nearly killed me.

I was skipping school most days, just sitting in the house. If mum came home from work early, I'd just go and sit quietly in my room. She never knew I was up there. Or I'd sneak out the front door and go and play in the garages at the back of me. Or take my ball and play Kirby on my own. If Craig came back early, I'd just tell him I got sent home unwell. He wasn't bothered – it was an afternoon of sex with me for him. But one day we nearly got caught by one of my sisters. I didn't hear Craig come in – as I was listening to music. He came into my room, didn't ask why I had come home, just told me to bend over the bed and pull my knickers down. I did as I was told as always. The Pet Shop Boys were playing on the radio and I was singing the words whilst he fucked me. But because the music was on, he didn't hear anyone else come in either. Next thing, "Craig are you in?" was shouted upstairs. He pulled out of me, told me to shut the fuck up and went out of my room leaving me lying there. "Yeah, just in the bathroom," he shouted. He sneaked into the bathroom, flushed the toilet then walked downstairs. I burst into tears – why had he done that? Why had he just left me without saying he loved me or what a good girl I was for Daddy? He swore at me and I was mortified. I got up and locked my door. I must have been crying so hard that my sister heard. "Emma," she said tapping on my door, "are you OK?" Next thing Craig is there too. "I've just smacked her," he said, "so she's kicking off. Caught her wagging school so gave her a good hiding." My sister shouts through the door, "You're such an idiot, Emma, when you gonna grow up?"

When my sister had gone back down, Craig came and knocked on the door and said, "Stop crying before your Mum gets back," and he pushed a 50p piece under the bottom of the door. "Go get yourself some sweets," he said. Then I didn't think about that 50p. Now I do – he was paying me to keep quiet, paying to have sex with me, like I was a child prostitute. I think about that 50p quite often and it always makes me feel ashamed, dirty, guilty and hatred towards the man who took my childhood off me. Then, I still had no clue what was going on or that it was wrong.

Jane and Susan started coming around and skipping school with me. We would just spend the day in bed touching each other and listening to music. Until one day the truant officer came to the house – Mum went crazy. How dare I tarnish her reputation blah blah blah, so I had to go back to school. I was terrified walking up to the school gates. I didn't have cigarettes if they wanted them, I could laugh because I was scared, and I was back in full uniform looking like an idiot. I had nothing to offer. I got towards the gym and Anna, one of the hard girls, shouted to me. I went over and it was like she was my best friend, asking me where I'd been and why I hadn't been in school. We chatted until the bell went – "See you at break," she said. How bizarre – the girl that made everyone be horrible to me was now being lovely to me. It turned out she had fallen out with the other hard girl and turned everyone against her, so she wanted everyone on her side including me.

Could I be nasty to someone else knowing how it feels? Knowing how frightened I was that I wouldn't even go to school but then a thought came in my head. One day before I started skipping school – when they were all being nasty to me – this girl came into the toilet whilst I was there. Just me and her. She told me that she did like me and she would talk to me but she had to pretend she hated me and gave me shit when Anna was around. I told her – "No", if she couldn't speak to me all the time, don't bother at all. And she never – she would just give me shit. So why should I care how she feels, she didn't care about me when I was being kicked and slapped with rulers.

I'd get called a slut by the boys but that was the one thing about the bullying that didn't bother me – what was a slut and why I was one. I used to think they weren't very sexually active. I remembered back to what Craig said about little dicks and them not being grown up. Craig was right – everyone I slept with did have a little dick. I couldn't even feel that they were having sex with me. I couldn't feel them inside me, not like Craig, I could feel him every time. I used to hurt to a point where my stomach would hurt and I'd bleed but not with any of the boys my age. It didn't last very long and I couldn't feel it, so who were they to call me a slut when they couldn't even fuck properly.

Things in school were good. I was popular again and the class clown. I always made people laugh either being cheeky or disruptive. The other girl who everyone had turned on, left the school. She couldn't take the abuse she got. She moved school and I never saw her until years later. I bumped into her and she was like a different person – well-spoken, seemed very loving and kind. Another one I'm glad that turned out OK. There were about 15 of us boys and girls that used to hang about together. The ones that people walk past with their heads down because they would get some kind of insult thrown at them.

One of the lads was different. He was actually nothing like us but for some reason fitted in. He was funny but lived in a nice area and his parents had good jobs. He asked us if we wanted to wag school at his house the following day. He told us that his mum and dad would be out all day and they had loads of beer. Only five of us went – me, another girl and three lads. His house was on an estate – ex-army houses they all looked the same with a huge green of overgrown grass in the middle – it came past your knees. You could lay on the floor and crawl through and no one would see you. There were some swings and a slide at the end of the long grass and a small park that had not been cared for.

We went into his house, played some music and started drinking." What do you want?" he said. They had every spirit you could think of, all unopened. What was the point in having all that, if you weren't going to drink it? I went straight for the whisky, it was the only one I recognised as that's what my nanna drank quite a lot of. In her last years, to be fair, she could sup a bottle a day and I know that because I used to have to go get it her from the shop. Back then, you could get a note off your parents or grandparents and go to the shop and get alcohol or cigarettes, everybody knew each other. Imagine doing that today – sending your 11-year-old to the shop with a note – but things were different back then.

Anyway, I asked for the whisky, thinking I was clever. What became of me was not fun and not clever. We had arrived at his house around 9.15 am and started to drink around 10.30 am. His parents were due home at half two, so we had to be cleaned up by then and be out of the house. So, we all decided when we were finished, we would go to the park and carry on drinking. We were all having such a good time and the girl that was with me decided to go upstairs with one of the boys. They had been gone a while, so we all sneaked upstairs and crept up on them. We opened the door and they were having sex. We were all laughing so much. We continued to drink and drink and the more we drank the sillier we became, but unlike my first time of head-spinning and having to lie down, this time I was elevated. I was really enjoying being drunk and we were all having a good laugh.

We went up to the top of the stairs again. This time not to spy on the ones having sex but for our next party trick. Once at the top, we proceeded to lie down, arms stretched out in front of us, and slide to the bottom. It was hilarious, over and over we continued, taking it in turns, making a funny trembling vibrating sound each step we went down. We were all paralytic – completely and utterly wasted. Next thing it's 2.20pm, his mum would be home from work soon. The house was a mess and there were people having sex upstairs. Everyone went into panic – apart from me of course – I was far too drunk to care.

His mum was a nurse – luckily for me – she saved my life. We got out of the house with minutes to go before she came home. We made our way through the long grass, most of that spent crawling on my hands and knees. I needed the toilet, so I just pulled my knickers down and started to wee in front of all my friends. We ended up reaching the park – I couldn't stand up, my eyes were rolling in my head. My friends tried to keep me upright, propped against the slide, but I was falling everywhere. One of my cousins, who wasn't really my cousin, came around the corner, walked over and asked what was up with me. "She is steaming," they said. He told them I was putting it on and proceeded to push me. I fell straight backwards, cracking my head on the concrete floor, eyes in the back of my head.

Our friend's mum had just pulled up and everyone was screaming and panicking. She came over, cleared my airways, put me in the recovery position and rang an ambulance. I was in a coma for three days. I had alcohol poisoning and had to have my stomach pumped. She saved my life – none of the kids would have known what to do, but she was so cross with her son for letting us in the house in the first place and he was that scared for when his dad came home. He locked himself in the downstairs toilet with his quilt and a packet of biscuits for three days, waiting to hear the news that I had come out of my coma. When I went back to school, we all laughed about the quilt and biscuits and have done a few times since.

When I woke up in the hospital, I was still drunk. I was walking around the ward with my gown wide open showing everyone my bottom, whilst I was trying to talk to the other kids who took an instant dislike to me. They actually hated me – as I realised when I woke the following day, after the nurses managed to get me back into bed to sleep it off. I opened my eyes the following morning to all eyes on me. I sat up in bed and the nurse came over. "What am I doing here?" I asked. She told me I had been in a coma for three days and my stomach had been pumped. I asked her where my mum was, and she said she had to ring her when I had woken from the coma. I sat there all day – no one came, and no one would talk to me, no matter how hard I tried. With all the kids on the ward, they would just tell me to go away. I can't blame them – they were all in with serious conditions and I'd got myself pissed, banged my head and ended up in a coma, taking a bed that I didn't deserve. 'When's my mum coming?' I would ask the nurses. "Don't know," they said. "We can't get hold of her."

Just after teatime, Craig walked in. I was relieved to see him. I smiled at him and he just shook his head. He got me up and told me we were walking home from the hospital as a punishment – about five or six miles. It wasn't punishment – we stopped in the field halfway for a finger and a blow job. And he hugged me – how was that punishment? We walked down our path. "Mum in?" I asked. "Yep," he said. I opened the back door and she was stood ironing in the kitchen with a cig hanging out of her mouth. I looked at her and she turned and said out of the corner of her mouth, "Don't do it again." I stood there speechless just looking at her. Was that it, was that all I got for being in a coma, for being in hospital? Was she not angry? Was she not furious about what I had done? Nope, just don't do it again.

I went upstairs, got changed, walked downstairs and past both of them. "I'm off out," I said but they didn't reply. I went to call on my friends which was a lot harder before technology, so you would walk to the nearest friend, knock on their door, is so and so coming out? She's not in, OK, thank you, then walk to the next house. Unless you had planned in school before you left, they could be anywhere and there were no mobile phones. I'd been in hospital for four days, so I'd made no arrangements. It could take two or three hours walking around every house or every park or shops to find someone. I eventually found them at the shops, everyone was so pleased to see me and of course, I was pleased to be with them. "What did your mum say, how come you're out, aren't you grounded?" "No, she doesn't give a shit, does she?"

Knowing I could do what I wanted and there were no boundaries or rules in my house, I started staying out and just going to school from wherever I'd stayed. I'd nip home at lunch, take my pizza and put it in the bin, then Mum would think I had been home after school at least. She probably never even checked but I thought that was a clever way of her thinking I must have been there. We all started hanging around another area of town and I met this boy. He was four years older than me, really naughty and I took a fancy to him instantly. We started going out as we would say. I really fell for him – he was my first crush, the first person I thought about constantly. He was tall with blonde hair.

He didn't meet me one night, as planned, so I went around and knocked on his door. His mum answered, told me he wasn't allowed out, he was grounded. Just as I was leaving, he came to the window in his PJs with racing cars printed all over them and told me to go and wait by the shops – he was going to sneak out. He came, we found a house to go to and had sex. We never really had private sex back then – there was always someone else in the bed next to you or just sat on a chair opposite. No one could see anything obviously – I'd just lie there thinking about something else, as always, and they would be on top of you for a minute and it was over. He didn't go to school – he went to a centre for naughty kids. I would wag school again and go and meet him. At the end of the street where his centre was, there was a pool hall. You could go in and hang about all day. There was a guy running it called Mark who was as dodgy as anything. He asked me if I wanted a tattoo. "Do I want a tattoo," I said to my boyfriend, "I'm only 11." "Yeah, have my initial on you," so I did, right slap bang in the middle of my arm. A huge S – he didn't do it with proper equipment so there was nothing sterile about it. Basically, it was with a needle and Indian ink. Scott, the boyfriend, was so pleased – we were inseparable for about 3 months, but it fizzled out and I was heartbroken, but imagine me in my first year of high school, aged 11 with a home-made tattoo. It made the cool kids think I was great, but the posh kids must have thought I was a mess. I was.

Towards the end of our first term, we started having sex education lessons, the kids laughing when certain words were mentioned like penis and vagina. Why were we having these lessons? Why were we being told about sexual things? We all knew them – we had been brought up with them. I knew more about Sex than History or English or Math. What a waste of time, I thought. They're sitting here teaching us things we all know about.

There was another production going on in the drama unit, but this time I didn't attend. I was addicted to nicotine – had to smoke every day and was now more interested in boys than music. The music teacher bumped into me in the corridor – "You need to come, Emma, you're so talented." But I couldn't, I wasn't losing my friends again. I was happy now, I couldn't commit to another drama project.

The truant officer had visited our house again and back then your parents were put on report. In school, there were three different ones, white report was an attendance report so basically you had to turn up at every lesson and get it signed by the teacher just to prove you had been in lesson, then yellow report that was for silly behaviour and attendance, then red report for naughty kids. You had to go and report to the Head every break for him to read the comments the teacher had made. I started on white but spent most of my time on red. You had to take it home for your parents to sign and comment on, then the teachers would read your parents' comments and so on and so on until all parties felt like behaviour had improved. As I wasn't really seeing my parents, I had to forge the report every night, always writing nice things about myself, of course.

One day in school one of my mates asked me if I wanted to go into town to have a walk around and check out the talent. We walked around and bumped into a few lads with a girl who was also called Emma. She was beautiful – long, wavy, blonde hair. She didn't speak like us, but she was funny and I hit it off with her straight away. By the end of the night, we had arranged to meet the next day. It was the weekend and I got up, bathed, got ready and walked into town to meet her. We ended up walking another four miles to her area of town, really posh big houses and golf courses. It was stunning. We met up with some more of her friends – everything was different. They didn't smoke or drink they just chilled, talking or listening to music. It was a different world – I'd never seen or been around people like this. These are the people we bully in school, I thought, but they were really nice. We went back to her house for tea. Both her parents were there. We were greeted as soon as we walked through the door – "Hello, beautiful," they said to Emma, "how's your day been?" She went over, gave them both a hug, then they introduced themselves to me. "Lovely to meet you," they said, "we've heard a lot about you." We had dinner – they had made a casserole with big spongy bits on top. "What's this?" I whispered to Emma. "Dumplings – they're lovely, try them." We had dinner, then a cake that her mother had baked, then we all went out into the garden and played swing ball together. I had a swing ball at home. I'd got it for Christmas one year, but I thought you played it on your own. I would hit the ball around and hit it back to myself. I didn't know it was a game for two people because there was only me all the time. it was such fun at Emma's house I didn't want to leave. Her parents dropped me off at home and we arranged a sleepover at hers for the following night. I was so excited, I couldn't sleep.

I got up the following morning, went downstairs – Mum was there. "What are you doing here?" I asked. "I'm off today – we are going down the coast in Wales. We're buying a caravan." "OK," I said, "well, I'm just going to meet my friend, I won't be long," and I walked out. When I got to

Emma's, it was just like the day before – we were all laughing, we played some board games, ate some great food and all sat down to watch a movie. After the film, we went upstairs, got into bed and fell asleep. The next day they dropped me off at home early to get ready for school. Mum was there again. "We've bought a caravan and we're going on holiday on Friday." I had arranged a sleepover at Emma's again, but now I couldn't go – I had to go on holiday with these two.

We arrived at the caravan. I thought it was amazing – we were in North Wales surrounded by funfairs, amusements, candy floss, fresh donuts. I'd never seen anything like it in my life. We unpacked everything after our bus ride – Mum and Craig didn't drive – but it didn't take us too long to get there anyway. About an hour and a half on the Coastliner, that's what the double-decker bus was called. Our caravan was the fourth one in, on the last row, next to everything that was exciting for me. I was eager to get out, so mum gave me £2 and told me not to come back till teatime.

I started walking towards the road – there was a fish and chip shop, then amusement arcades. Opposite was a bar where all the entertainment went on. The last place was prize bingo, there was a railway track next to the prize bingo and you had to stop to look both ways and run across before any trains came. On the other side of the track was a funfair and the beach, the entire place was owned by one family and their house was next to the bar – a beautiful white bungalow. They had a son, Luke, who was gorgeous. I wanted him to notice me as soon as I saw him. Sometimes he would work on the waltzes, his lovely blonde hair falling on his face, as he pushed people around. The music was loud, and I would stand there on my own staring at him. All around the waltzes were groups of girls staring at him, I didn't stand a chance really – here was me, 11 years old, my hair in a ponytail, goofy teeth and matching t-shirt and leggings.

I spent most of my time in the arcade on my first day there, there was a video game called Pac land and I was addicted, it was 10p a go and I'd soon spent my £2. It wasn't near teatime – I had only been there a couple of hours and I had no money left but I couldn't go back to the caravan. Mum told me I could only go back at teatime, so I wandered around on my own, looking at the sights. I never felt afraid – I felt like I belonged there. I was watching a boy play a machine and we got talking. He was with his brother who was a bit of a nutcase, but they were funny and really nice to me. I ended up walking around with them for a few hours until it was five-thirty. "I've got to go back now," I said, "for my tea." So we planned to meet at seven in the arcade where we'd first met. I went back to the caravan and it was locked – no one was there, so I had to go and find Mum and Craig.

It was getting dark and I hadn't eaten all day and I was getting a little anxious because I didn't know where they were. I walked over to the bar because there was an artist singing, I thought they could have been watching her performance, but they weren't there. I looked around the amusements, they were nowhere to be found, so I was just walking around on my own. For about an hour and a half. As I was walking back down, I thought about the bingo – maybe they were in there, so I walked down and yes, there they were drinking tea, playing for points to win prizes like a pan set or an ashtray. "What are you doing?" I asked, "I'm hungry, can we go get some dinner?" She gave me another £2, told me to get some chips from the chippy and bugger off. So, I went and got some chips, sat on the wall outside the amusements and waited for my new friends to come back – Lee and Scott. I fancied Lee he was a nice-looking lad with a good sense of humour, but he never really showed me he was interested in me in a sexual way. Not then anyway.

I got back to the caravan around midnight – Mum was in the bedroom, Craig in the living room. I went over to the sofa, sat down – he didn't say anything, didn't ask how my night had been, just said, "Alright?" I said, "Yeah, did you win anything at bingo?" He told me that it didn't work like that and you had to save up your points to get something good at the end of the week. Something good – the place was full of shit and the amount of money you spent trying to win something good, you could have gone to the shop and bought it. I had to suck his penis that night – it was making me be sick in my mouth, as it plunged to the back of my throat. I'm there sucking him off, choking whilst Mum's in the next room. He's saying, good girl for Daddy in a caravan and my mum's not hearing anything. What a load of shit she was, lying there, reading a book and not hearing anything through the 5cm wall, 10 meters from where she was.

The next day and every day we were there, I had the same routine – get up, get £2, come back at half five, go the bingo and get another £2, go out with Lee and Scott and then come back whenever I wanted. Lee and Scott lived there, and Lee worked part-time in a bar up the road, so I'd go and sit on the wall and wait for him to finish some nights then we would go walking or to one of his friend's houses and smoke pot. I had a great time that holiday and cried all the way home on the Coastliner. When we got back from North Wales I hated being at home. I couldn't stand being around them, that feeling of Craig fucking me or him even near me, even him breathing made me mad. All I thought about was Lee. I was starting to get breasts and my mood was all over the place and my attitude stank. I couldn't get in touch with Emma and wanted to see her, but every time I went to the place that we met in town she was never there, and I couldn't go to her house it was too far away, so I went back to my old ways, staying out, having sex and partying.

A few weeks later we went on another caravan holiday. I think they only took me because they had to this time. My sister Mel came with me — there was a Morris Dancing competition going on and we all had to be there. We had separate caravans, of course, one for me and my sister and a cousin and one for Mum and Craig. I kept thinking I wasn't too far from where we stayed last time — only a few hours down the road, I could walk and see Lee. But that never happened, I'd planned to go see him, just turn up outside his work — he would be pleased to see me, surely.

In the afternoon, we were sat outside the caravan and I had terrible stomach ache. "Go to the toilet," my sister said. She would have been 13 at the time. I went to the toilet, pulled down my knickers and there was blood everywhere. I was so frightened, I started screaming, I was crying hysterically. My sister came rushing in. "What's the matter?" she said. "I've cut myself, I don't know where, I can't find it." She looked at me and told me I had started my periods. "What the fuck is that and why do I have bright red blood in my knickers and down my legs?" She told me to wait on the toilet and she would go and get Mum who would explain everything. I sat there for almost half an hour, still crying and just Mel came, "Give me your knickers," she said. "Mum doesn't believe me." I took off my knickers and gave them to her, off she went again. She came back with a £5 note and told me I had to go in the shop and buy sanitary pads, they would be by all the shampoo and bubble bath, then come back, get changed and put one of those pads in my knickers. I should change it every few hours and flush the dirty one down the toilet. I asked her what was going on and she just said bathe because you will smell – it happens to every girl, don't worry about it.

So off I went to the shop with tissue in my knickers to protect me. I walked up and down the toiletry aisle until I found a big white packet with red writing on. I took them to the counter, paid for them, took them home, exchanged my tissue for this huge pad. I was walking with my legs wide apart it was so uncomfortable, and I still had no idea what was happening. All I knew was I couldn't go to see Lee like this, I looked a mess.

3:

It All Comes Out in The Wash

When I went back to school after my traumatic holiday, I was still very confused. I felt different, I had hair under my armpits and on my legs and I was still having to deal with this blood issue. Our first lesson was PE and we were playing rounders. I hated rounders, it was so boring. I couldn't bat or bowl or catch or throw so I'd just be a spare part on the field. They always used to place me as far back as possible, because they knew no one would hit it that far and I could just stand there for an hour doing nothing which I was pretty good at.

After rounders, we all had to shower. There was one long shower room and everybody had to share. I remember getting undressed and for the first time feeling uncomfortable. I had these hairs everywhere and little boobs and I couldn't see anyone else with them. I pulled my knickers down to reveal this pad and left it on the floor with the rest of my clothes whilst I went into the shower, trying to cover up these things no one seemed to have. We were just about to leave the shower room when the PE teacher shouted me back. "Emma, can I have a word?" she said. I went and sat in the changing room and she sat next to me looking quite embarrassed. "Has your mother not written you a note for PE?" "No," I replied. "When you're on your period, Emma, you can't shower, and it is not right that you just left your underwear there with a dirty pad in." "What am I meant to do with it then?" I asked. "Your mother has obviously gone through with you what is happening to you, hasn't she?" I started to cry and explained to her I had no clue what was happening to me. I was just told to buy these pads. She leant over, hugged me and said, "Come with me." She took me to her office and explained why I was bleeding and why it was a necessary part of life for women so they could have babies in the future. "How do you have babies?" I said. "Are you taking sex education lessons?" I nodded. "So, you have been told about the penis and vagina?" I told her I had, but I already knew what a penis and vagina were. She smiled at me, "Well don't worry about it, Emma, you have lots of time to try and understand it – you're only little."

I walked away feeling better that I understood a bit more. The only thing I didn't get was why I had plenty of time for what. What I did know was, I was good at forging notes off my mum. I'd been filling in my own report, so every time PE came around I'd write a note with reasons why I couldn't do it. I was too ashamed to get undressed. When I was in my room that night Craig came in as usual. "You still on that period?" he said. "Yes, I am, the teacher taught me about them today. I will be bleeding anywhere between five and seven days," I said proudly. "Just suck my dick then and let me know when you've stopped." Why did I have to let him know when I'd stopped? There was obviously more I needed to learn. I paid careful attention in sex education classes after my talk with the PE teacher. I didn't know why I would understand more when I was older when I understood so much already. She had just smiled at me when I told her I knew what a vagina was, and a penis but why did she tell me I was only little, and I had plenty of time? I didn't understand so I thought I would get my answers from my lessons. But I never did. They continued to tell us that you could have babies if you had sex but that surely that didn't happen until you were old like my mum. What they were teaching us didn't make sense. I couldn't have babies – I was still a child myself. Yes, I was drinking and staying out and being rebellious but every night that I was at home I was still playing with my dolls. I was still playing happy families with Sindy, even if I had been out the night before and got drunk and had sex, I still needed my dolls they were important to me.

I always wanted a farm when I was little – a toy one with loads of animals. I love animals, I am ashamed of most of the things I have done in my past, ashamed of all the things I have done and the people I have abused and I'm ashamed of the people I have slept with thinking it was OK, but I could never be more ashamed of the one thing I have been trying not to write about. But if I don't write about it, I'm not being true to myself or being open and honest, as I swore I would be when I started this. I'd still be hiding something, I'd still be needing to get more out of my soul and I'd still be living in the past because I couldn't let go of the shame.

When I talk about things, when I say them out loud, it's real. I feel I'm letting go of a demon – one more thing that's out. One more experience I can heal, one more fucked-up thing that my family put me through, one more time I said OK, but it wasn't. My last time of saying OK. I have continued my whole life trying to please people, even in situations that have been hard for me, because I have still tried to please everyone but me. My latest attempt at a relationship ended after 28 days, and I didn't speak to him for fourteen of those. I froze. I hated myself after two weeks. He took me to a Swingers club – he was a friend beforehand, someone I played pool with – but he was very good to me, looked after me when I was sad, came to the hospital with me when I had my breakdown, sat with me for hours so I thought it was someone that really cared for me. I told him I liked dirty sex because it didn't remind me of anything but it wasn't true, it was because we never had normal sex, so once again I went along with it and tried to please another fucking man.

I got told I just laid there once, when I was younger, and that I didn't do anything, well I'm sorry but I didn't realise I had to do anything. I didn't realise it was a two-way thing, I didn't realise I was meant to enjoy it as well. I've spent my whole life getting fucked by people and being told just to sit there and keep my mouth shut. I've spent years thinking I was here to please a man, make them happy, I've spent my whole life judging myself, trying to be perfect to please other people so going to a Swingers' club and having sex with your partner whilst another dirty bastard pervert was stood there wanking, having sex every night but using poppers to get that rush. What the hell is wrong with me, why did I put myself in that situation again? I felt dirty, the whore I used to be, when all I want in this world is for someone to see me for what I am and just me, without the dirtiness, without sexual aids. Just for someone to look at me whilst they're making love to me and for me to feel it's OK, before I just fuck this whole sex lark off because I can't take it anymore. Why doesn't anyone understand me, when I try to reach out? Why can't my vulnerability be endearing? Why do I always have to be something I'm not, someone I don't want to be? Who is ever just going to love me, strip me back layer by layer and like who I really am without the pretence? Who is going to make me feel safe? Who is ever going to let me be myself and stay?

I'm difficult, I know, I'm difficult. I clam up, I can't speak when I'm confronted with things when I behave irrationally and I'm asked about it. I just sit there – I'm not being awkward, I can't tell a man how I feel. I just go in my own head – thinking, not saying anything – thinking it will all go away but I'm only like this because I'm scared. I'm frightened because I can't think normally like most people. I still don't care about myself enough to be happy with how I deal with situations. I'm vulnerable and I still can't say no. I want someone in my life to build me up, to allow me to pull back, to allow me to feel OK when I'm feeling sad. Someone strong enough to be able to see I'm having a bad day and it's not their fault. Why do people always think there's something wrong with you or they have done something to you on days where I am just struggling just being me? I don't want to think about these things, but I want more than anything to explain how it feels, to finally get it out there. The damage doesn't just happen and you forget about it, it never goes away, and this is me dealing with it for the first time, talking about it because I don't want another woman or man feeling like this for thirty-four years and believing they're on their own because they're not. I can't be fucking happy all the time, all this coming out of me is painful. It's difficult to sit here and write about things I didn't ever think would come back into my head, let alone my lips! What is wrong with wanting someone to please me, to understand my pain, to see that I'm re-living it all over again, that I need patience, I need nurturing, I need to feel safe? Why can't someone see me for that? See through my bullshit, see through the pain and hurt I have locked away for so long. See me – I just want someone to see me. But why would anyone want me, why would anyone want someone who sleeps with animals? Who would want that?

When I was on my period, Craig brought our cat in the room one night and made me take my knickers down. He pushed the cat towards me, Craig was staring straight into my eyes. "It's OK," he said, "you will be clean soon, clean enough for Daddy to fuck you." I could feel every lick, the rough tongue of my pet, my friend, licking away at my period. I froze and had tears coming down my cheeks – why does my cat have to do this, why is my Daddy making my best friend do this to me? Craig held the cat from behind stroking him to make sure he felt safe. I could hear him purring and Craig moaning. Lick by lick, my friend ate away at me, happy and content and Craig's moans still play through my head. Every time I think of them, they get louder and louder. It seemed to last for ages, I felt. I was sat there, legs wide open blood dripping down my legs and my cat happily purring. Then he just put the cat out the way – "You're clean enough for Daddy now, good girl you're such a good girl." Then he put himself inside me and fucked me as I lay there in shock, not understanding what had just happened.

It is the hardest thing I have to think about, when I have to sit and go over it in my head. It was probably the time I started storing things in my memory – the road that led me to being unsure about myself, the road that I continued to take where I had no self-worth. 45 years old and with all the relationships in my adult life, I have never made love. How does that feel? I have never had someone be gentle and loving in my bed? How does it feel to be loved? I know I thought I had loved at the beginning of the year, but had I? As I continue this journey of self-discovery, I think again it was more about someone being nice to me and me grabbing on to that. I didn't respect myself even then – at a time I thought I was so happy. I was trying to please him again. As I said right at the very beginning, it wasn't about us breaking up that made me breakdown, it was about the rejection. I never give up hoping there is someone out there for me, who will love me, but how many times do I have to keep trying? How many times do I have to feel worthless and please other people? Isn't it fair for someone to please me? Am I such a bad person? Can I not be loving and nice without feeling like I have to please someone? Is there such a thing as working together and wanting the same things, loving each other equally?

Apparently, there is someone out there for everyone, but I can't settle any more for anything less than I deserve and need, because I can't please another man, I can't do it. The man I thought loved me, the man I thought I loved knew things about me – I'd told him bits, not everything, but it put me off telling another living soul. My experience with him now feels like the beginning of my book, the start of me falling to pieces. At the time we split, I was sad. As the months have passed, reality has sunk in – he never thought about me as he said, and I was too blind to see it. I was just letting someone that told me I was beautiful inside and out and thought I was funny, blind me. This man told me he was going to fetch his friends round to rape me. As one of his sexual fantasies, he would ask me which one of his friends I would want. I'd tell him, I just want you, and he would say come on tell me who would you like to rape you whilst I watch? He wanted me to be his little girl and he was my Daddy. He put on a porn film of him and his ex-wife and we watched it. I cried myself to sleep. I know in my heart these things were not in any way nasty, they were fantasies and I'm OK with that. If I hadn't been through what I have, I might not have thought twice about them, but instead, I went into myself again. Overthinking everything, feeling dirty and unloved. And that is where I lost him. He told me I had changed and I wasn't fun anymore.

I used to go to sleep thinking about the things he told me. I know he would never have wanted me to feel dirty or uncomfortable, but he knew about me and he continued to have his fantasies and I continued to accept it like always. I am a very strong person who has been abused and feels inferior to a man, who still thinks she has to please them, to make them happy when all it has done is destroy my soul. Writing about all this is making me a stronger person and I am going to be able to say No by the end of this and I am going to believe I am worthy of all the things I want. I'm not looking for another relationship – I can't let myself hurt me anymore. I have to find out who I am and care enough about myself to not let anyone make me feel anything else but good about myself. I have such a hard time believing that and trying to forgive myself for everything I have done. I don't need someone who can put me down.

One day someone will see this loving caring person who acts as a hard-faced woman that doesn't give a shit and just wants a laugh. When he sees me, I mean really sees me and laughs with me and wants to make love to me, even knowing my past, maybe I will pay attention but until then, I'm flying solo. Sleeping with my cat was probably the turning point in my life. For the first time in all the years with the different men and boys and girls I had been sexually active with, I knew it was wrong, I knew that pets were not meant to lick you in your private parts. I'd never had sexual thoughts towards my animals, like I did with my Daddy or boys in school. I'd never looked at my dog and thought I want to wank you. I was completely stunned, but I couldn't stop thinking about it and it made me start questioning everything else. Other girls were having sex at my age so surely, they must know all about it from growing up – they must have liked sex or why else would they be having it? I knew we weren't allowed to talk about the sex we had at home, that was drilled into me, we would lose each other because Craig would have to get a new girl if I told, because he wouldn't be nice to me anymore. Then Mum would be cross, and I would have no one to love me.

Things continued pretty horrible for the next few weeks. Craig bringing the cat in and me once again just lying there, staring at the ceiling, hoping it would end soon. My behaviour worsened – I was being naughty in school, was on red report every day. I was rebelling against something, but I didn't know what. I hated everybody and anybody, I went out one night with my friends, it was pretty late by the time we had all had a drink and a mess about, maybe 2 am, maybe later. We were walking past the local dairy, all the milk floats outside, and we thought it would be a good idea to take one. We sneaked in, pushed it out of the dairy not to disturb anyone and started it up on the main road, two lads in the front and two girls in the back. We couldn't stop laughing – us, these little kids, driving round the streets at stupid o'clock in the morning. We lasted about an hour before we turned into a road with a huge hill. We were trying to get the float up the hill but it was too steep. Next thing we heard sirens from the police. We all jumped out with the milk float going backwards! We heard it crash and continued running up the hill, my heart pounding. I was scared but it was exciting, I was excited about the thrill of what we had done.

The next day when I went up town, I went into a shop and stole some pens, I got away with it. Through stealing, I met up with some older girls who were really good at it. I was taking colouring pens and postcards from an art shop that used to make me smile when I walked around it, all the different colours it looked so pretty, but the older girls were stealing clothes and shoes. "Come with us, Emma, we can get you a new pair of shoes." I agreed, I had been a shoplifter for less than a week and here I was going in shops stealing things that were expensive. Well, at least that's what I thought I would be doing. "I'll show you how to do it," she said. Back then all the shoes were out, not just one like today and you have to ask for your size. You could just walk in and take a brand-new pair so we walked in and over to the shoes. She decided which ones she wanted – they were black, patent, pointy toes with a five-inch heel. She took off her old shoes placed them on the shelf and just walked out, as easy as that. She told next day would be my turn, so I arranged to meet her at 2pm – the shops were busy then, I walked in with my shitty attitude but I had newish shoes on and I didn't want to leave them there, so I picked up the shoes placed them under my arm and headed for the door. My first big steal! I had new shoes, but not for long. As soon as I walked out of the door, someone's hand was on my shoulder and they told me they were a store detective and I had to go back in the shop because they had just witnessed me stealing. I went and sat in this little room and they asked me why I had stolen them, I just sat there quite cocky and ignored them. I was there for about 25 mins, then the police turned up, read me my rights and marched me out of this big store in the middle of the town centre everyone staring at me. When I got down the police station, they took my fingerprints and my photo and put me in a cell. They couldn't interview me because I was a minor and my parents or guardian had to be there. Good luck with that I thought, I was going to rot there.

As I sat in my cell I was really frightened, but I was going to show that I was one of the hard kids – the big guns – and when Mum turned up, she would only say don't do it again anyway. But she never came, neither did Craig – it was my eldest sister. They had placed me in an interview room, I was sat in the chair with my arm over the back of it, slouching, chewing gum, when my sister Sharon walked in. She was horrified – "Sit up," she demanded, "and get rid of that chewing gum, you're a disgrace to the family." I sat up, eyes rolling at her, whilst they talked to me. They left me in there with her for ages. I would have rather been talked to by the police than her, she never shut up about how stupid I was, and how disappointed she was in me. I was just looking at her, thinking shut up, you dickhead. I was given a caution – the only one I have ever had, the only time I have ever been in trouble with the police. Maybe what she said had an effect on me or maybe what was yet to come saved me.

I started spiralling into a deep depression – all I could think about was how bad I was, how everyone treated me, what was happening with Craig and Tabby. I'd not seen Jane or Susan for a while, they just stopped coming. My head was all over the place and I didn't want to be here anymore. I was sat in my locked bedroom thinking of ways to escape – I didn't think about death at that point – I just wanted to get away, so I hatched a plan. I went downstairs took Mum's caravan keys, took money out of her purse and armed with a carrier bag full of clothes made my way to the bus stop to wait for the Coastliner. It came and there I was on a bus, on my own, excited about my new life. I was going to get to see Lee and the other friends I'd made in North Wales. I was going to be free and happy. I would show them I was OK, I didn't need anyone.

When I got there, I opened up the caravan, sat there for a few minutes, counted the money I had stolen and I had exactly £10.50 left. That was a lot of money to me, I would be OK, I thought. I put my clothes away and went straight to Lee's and knocked on the door. Nobody was in, so I started my hunt for him, walking around all the arcades, going to his work. Nothing – I could not find him or his brother Scott. I eventually bumped into someone who told me they were on holiday and wouldn't be back for a few days. That was OK. I said, "We have just moved up here, we're staying in the caravan until we can find a house." I didn't want them to know I was on my own, so I pretended the whole family was up. It was in the height of season and it was really busy, one of the girls I got to know who was 14 was working in a donut parlour part-time and making between £10 and £15 a week, so I used to go and sit and talk to her in the day. She would give me free burgers or hotdogs and donuts but pretty soon my money started to go, even if I was getting free food. I was spending money in the arcades and on the occasional packet of cigarettes when I could find someone to go into the shop for me. I'd been away for around five days and wondered if anyone had noticed I'd gone, wondered if I had been missed. I was living on my own and no one knew about it. I was having a whale of a time and when Lee came back of his holiday he was so pleased to see me he gave me a big hug and we went back to just how it used to be spending as much time together as we could, laughing. Scott ended up getting a little jealous because we were always together so we had to include him some more and he got over it.

I'd been living on my own in the caravan for around two weeks and only had a few pence left to my name so went around trying to find a job. I helped out in the donut parlour a couple of days a week and the rest of it I was selling jumpers on the market. I felt liberated, I was happy, my mood was lifting. I was living in a place where I was happy with people that didn't ask me for anything. I'd been living at the caravan for almost a month. Me and Lee became so close, although nothing sexual had happened, he was my friend, he was like my brother. One afternoon I had just finished work and was making my way back to the caravan to get changed to go and see Lee, but when I got there the door was open. Had someone broken in, had I left it open? I was sure I hadn't. I peered in – everything was still there. The place was a bit of a state, to be honest, but that was from me, nothing looked like it had been touched.

I ran across the walkway to another caravan and just stood there waiting to see what happened. I was there for over an hour and then I saw him, as soon as I saw his face I felt anger, rage – fuck off and leave me to be happy, I thought, but he stood there walking around and around the caravan. I was caught, he had come to get me – it had only taken a month! What could I do now? Everyone thought my parents were here – they didn't know I was on my own. I couldn't go now and tell them the truth, especially to Lee what would he think of me? I knew I had to see him again, I knew I couldn't go without saying goodbye. I went and knocked on his door for what was the final time. "I'm going," I said, "it's not working out for my parents up here, so we're going back." I was crying, he stood and looked at me, tears welling in his eyes. "Give me five mins," he said, I waited outside for him. We went and sat in his father's car and he kissed me, we hugged, that was the last time I ever saw Lee and his brother and every other person I had become friends with. I went back when I was in my thirties to see how it had changed, it hadn't, not much. I stood outside Lee's house and wondered if I should knock, wondered if he would remember me.

I got out of the car, tears rolling down my cheeks and thought – fuck you, Craig, you can wait a bit longer. I walked around saying bye to everyone and wanted to walk to all the places I had been with Lee. I went to climb over a fence to some field we had been walking in and because of the tears in my eyes, I fell. When I went to get up, I couldn't walk, my foot and ankle on the right-hand side were hurting. I limped all the way back to the caravan. When I got there, Craig had gone but I knew he wouldn't be far away so I collected my things together and just sat there waiting for him to come back. He walked in the caravan and said, "Your mum hates you." "Tell me something I didn't already know. I've hurt my ankle," I said. By this point, it was really swollen. "Your own fault," he said, "now get your stuff, I'm taking you home."

As I was getting my stuff together, I could hear the zipper on his trousers undoing. "Stop that for a minute, put this in your mouth." I got down on my knees and put his penis in my mouth. He had hold of my hair, pulling it really hard, slamming my face backwards and forwards on his penis choking me. I had tears flowing uncontrollably down both cheeks on my face. "What are you crying for?" he said, "you love it."

He didn't speak to me all the way home which was a good thing. I didn't want to talk to him either. I walked in the front door. Mum wasn't there – I went upstairs, cried myself to sleep. My mum never mentioned it – never brought it up, not to me anyway, but she did to someone else eventually. I'd been gone a month – they hadn't reported me missing to the police. I guess it must have taken them a while to notice I was gone anyway. I started to feel sad again, pretty quickly, but somehow, I'd grown up. I mean I was still 11 but I'd been working and looking after myself so well and I was eating so much better than I did at home.

I went back to school, but I was different – I was quiet. I still smoked and still do to this day, but it wasn't happy Emma, it wasn't the girl that made everyone laugh. I felt like I'd had the life sucked out of me, I would go home and lock my door straight away. I didn't want Craig near me and when he would come knocking on my door, I would pretend I was asleep. I was isolated and that's when I first thought about suicide, planning on killing yourself when you're 11. I didn't know how to, but I had heard about people talking about overdoses and how it could kill you. I learnt this from the chat shows Mum used to watch when she was at home.

I started opening drawer after drawer until I had about 50 paracetamol tablets. I went upstairs with a bottle of diet coke, sat on my bed and called for my friend Tabby. He came to me, purring, pushing his face against mine and I told him all about my journey and how sad I was. I apologised to him for everything Craig had made him do, but he was OK. He curled up on my knee and I sat looking at him. I could hardly breathe with tears and emotion, trying to explain I didn't hate him and that I loved him very much. I told him he was the best friend I'd ever had and I forgave him for the things he had done to me and begged him to forgive me for everything I put him through. I never meant to hurt him. Do animals think like us? Did I destroy him? Was he damaged, like me? Did I impose physical and mental scars on him? I spoke to him for over an hour, just crying, telling him how sorry I was and how I felt about things, how confused I was. I didn't know what was happening.

I must have been there for another hour, thinking about what I was about to do. I put Tabby on the floor and ushered him out of my room, locked the door, sat on the bed and took my tablets. I had had enough, I couldn't cope anymore, I didn't want to be there, I felt empty inside with a sickly feeling. I didn't feel a part of anything or anyone, no one would miss me, no one cared enough. I'd been away for a month, working on my own, no one missed me. The thought of being so young and so lonely and feeling different to other people. To grow up hiding your thoughts and fears to protect people that have destroyed you, to be in that place was enough. I'd had enough, and I was about to have my first suicide attempt, the first of many.

I couldn't even do that properly. I woke up feeling sick and dizzy. Why did I wake up? Why was I still here? I had nothing to offer apart from my used body and my unstable mind. I unlocked the door and Tabby was sat outside. He came bursting in and was purring around my legs. I sat back down and he jumped on my knee. It was daylight. I heard Craig come upstairs, he shouted to me as he went in his room, "You can't stay in there forever, stop being such a bitch." Forever!! What did he mean? I heard the back door go and Mum and Craig went out. I went downstairs, got some water and put the TV on? The Love Boat was on. I sat there for a few minutes and then realised what Craig meant. I took my tablets on Friday and the Love Boat is always on Sundays. I'd slept for two days. I'd lost two days of my life. If I had died, if it had worked, how long would I have been in that bedroom before they thought something was wrong? Did they think I was ignoring them? Did they even shout for me at all? Were they not bothered I hadn't eaten for days? Obviously not, I could have just rotted in that room. Tabby was the only one who cared – I bet he was outside my room the whole time, I bet he understood what I was saying to him and he was worried about me. As for Mum and Craig – what a joke!

My next thought was what was I to do now. I didn't want to be in this house one more day. I didn't want to be in this existence. I was the horror child – they actually made me believe that in later years. I got myself together and went up town, hunting for Emma, I was just about to give up looking for her and there she was walking down the street with another girl. I shouted to her and she looked pleased to see me, we spent a couple of hours talking and we arranged to meet the next day for a sleepover. I suddenly had something to live for. I was happy again, I went home, went straight to my room and locked the door.

The next day was to be the turning point I longed for, and should have had long before. I went to Emma's house and as before, her parents were so welcoming, they seemed really pleased to see me. We had dinner and played monopoly all together and then we went up to her room, I got undressed took off all my clothes and lay there. "Have you not got any PJs?" she said and there, at that moment, I just looked at her and said, "Yes, but I'll put them on when your dad has been in, what time does he come?" She asked me what I meant. I asked her if she got touched in her private parts by her Daddy. She told me to put my PJs on and told me to go to sleep. I lay there thinking about what I had said – maybe I shouldn't have said it like that. I should have rephrased it differently. I should have been more subtle – maybe she didn't like the thought of her dad touching me. Maybe she wanted him to herself, I thought. The last thought before I went to sleep was – I hope I don't lose my friend, I will apologise in the morning.

The next morning, I woke, and she was just staring at me. I started laughing. "What are you looking at?" I said. "Are you OK?" she said, looking concerned. "I'm OK, I'm so glad I have met up with you again." "You need to get dressed!" "Before breakfast?" I asked. "Yeah, just get dressed." So, I got up, went in the bathroom, washed my face and went back into her room, we were sat on the bed. "Are we not going down for breakfast?" "Yeah, in a minute." We just sat opposite each other on our single beds for about 10 minutes in complete silence. Next thing, "Emma, can you come downstairs and bring Emma with you." I walked downstairs and was greeted by her mum who was stood outside the closed living room door. She put her arms around me and told me that I had no reason to be frightened and that she was going to be by my side the whole time. I looked at her not having one clue what she meant. She told Emma to go in the kitchen with her dad, Emma hugged me so tight and off she went.

"Ready?" her mum said. I said, "Yes, ready for what?" I walked into the living room to be greeted by five or six people all in suits." "Ah, Emma," one of the ladies said, "come and have a sit down, would it be OK for us to have a chat?" "Yeah, sure, what about?" All eyes on me I could feel them all staring at me and I didn't like it. And so, it started, "Can you tell me about your relationship with your stepfather?" "He's nice to me," I said. "Can you tell me if he touches you in your private places?" "I can't answer that, I'm not allowed to," I replied. "Why are you not allowed to Emma, you are safe here and anything you say is OK no one's going to hurt you, so does he touch you and if so where?" I just pointed to my little breasts and my vagina. "Does he hurt you?" I started to cry, and then it all started coming out – I told her about my cat, I told her about his brother and what he had done. I asked her if I was in trouble, the whole time Emma's mum holding my hand. "You're not in trouble, sweetie," she said, "but I need you to come with us and talk through things again. Can you do that?" "Yes," I said.

I went outside the house and there were six cars parked outside, only one of them belonging to Emma's parents. I saw a police car and got afraid. "Are you going to lock me up again?" I asked. "No," she said, "we're going to look after you now and make you safe." I didn't go to the police station, I went to a house that was next to it, it was just like any other house, a kitchen, a living room, a bathroom, but there was also a room with two chairs in and a video camera and a room with a long bed like you saw at the hospital. They took me into the living room and told me what was going to happen next. She told me I was going to have to lie on the bed and a doctor was going to come and examine me which meant him putting his fingers inside me. "That's OK," I said. I was used to that. I remember the doctor having a white jacket on, like they used to in those days, very official. He seemed old and had grey hair and glasses. He started to examine me – it hurt a little – but not as much as when Craig was pushing Ben's hips backwards and forwards. We came out of that room, went back into the living room and I sat with Emma's mum. "You're doing really well," she said. I just smiled – still no real idea what was going on.

The police officer came back in. She was from a special unit in the police force – I remember her telling me that. She was very pretty with long brown flowing hair, she was the type of person that made you feel safe, her gentle voice and welcoming smile. I liked her from the offset. I can't remember her name but I can see her lovely smile. She continued to tell me that I was going to be videoed and I was going to be asked a lot of things which I thought I wasn't allowed to talk about, but I could answer them honestly and they were going to help me be OK and feel happy again. I walked into the room – just me and the lovely police officer. I sat on one chair with a camera on me, she sat opposite out of sight. The questions started. I described the wiry feeling I got when he was on top of me, how he would open up my little vagina and put as many fingers as he could in, how he would tell me how beautiful I was and that I was his princess. I continued on and on, I couldn't stop but also about everything that was nice about him. How lucky I was to have such a good Daddy but that I didn't like it when he brought my cat in the room. Every question I answered she smiled at me and told me how good I was doing. Unknown to me, while I was in this funny little house, the police had gone and arrested Craig. He was sat in the police station next door and I was in a house next to him. I was there the whole day – they told me they had more questions for me but I had done well for that day, and tomorrow I would have to do it all again. I was tired and drained and I agreed, and I waited there to be picked up by my mum. I hoped she wasn't mad with me – I'd told the truth and I had said what a good Daddy Craig was, but Mum never came, neither did Craig, nor my sister. A lady with a floral skirt and a farming jacket walked in. "Hello," she said, "I'm Francis, I'm a social worker and I'm going to look after you."

4:

Where Do I Belong?

Francis' car was messy and smelled of animals, and what the hell was a social worker? I sat there, giving her the occasional smile every now and then, thinking I don't want to live with you. She stank. We drove through the town centre and to what was known to me as the posh side of town, not where Emma lived but another area. All the houses were big with lovely gardens, the streets were well kept – no mess anywhere, nice cars parked in their driveways, I wondered where I was going! I can't see this smelly woman living around here I thought, so who is going to look after me – they have to be nice to live in an area like this, they will be like Emma's parents. I didn't feel afraid, I was actually looking forward to it. They are going to play games with me, I thought. I was sat in the car, smiling. "Are you OK?" said Francis. "Yes, I'm good, thank you. It's lovely around here, isn't it?" "Yes," she said, "you will be safe here." I was still not getting why I was going to be safe, not fully understanding what was going on. But at least I may be getting a decent meal tonight, I thought.

We turned off onto an estate of lovely little bungalows – my smile grew bigger. We turned down a lane, went through some gates. I could see two new build houses in front of me – they didn't fit in with anything around there. I thought that was strange, we turned to the left and the reality struck I was not going to a lovely home with nice parents. This looked like a community centre with bars on the windows. Surely, I was going here to speak to someone, not stay here. It was probably for more questions, more confusion. I got out of the car. This place didn't look nice or welcoming. Was it a community centre, I thought, but why were there bars on the windows? Was I going to prison? Craig did tell me I would get in trouble if I told anyone. I started to shake. "Am I going to prison?" I asked. "No," Francis replied. "We're just going to have a chat." Ahh – it was a community centre, I gave a sigh of relief.

The building was all on one level. Every window looked the same – it was in a huge L shape. We walked into a reception area. I was told to sit down and Francis disappeared. Half an hour went by and she came back and told me to come with her. I walked into an office with her and there was a lady sat there smiling at me. "Hello Emma," she said, "come in and have a seat."

So it began, she explained to me that I was in a children's home. "It's a place where kids go when it is not safe for them to be at home." I didn't like living at home but I didn't know I wasn't safe there. The look on my face must have been one of confusion. "Let's go get you settled and we will have a much longer chat." She told me the nice lady from the police station was coming to see me in a couple of hours. I got up and we walked through this building next to the offices. There was a huge area on one side with a snooker table and on the other what looked like a school canteen with two elderly ladies cooking, they smiled at me as I walked past. We got to a door and she had to unlock it, then another locked door. I was starting to feel very afraid. Where was I? Why were all the doors locked? Why was I here? I wanted to go home. I was shaking with fear and tears started rolling down my face. We got to another door and once again it had to be unlocked and locked behind us.

Here I was, stood in my new home. It was not pretty, as I had been imagining on the way there. A huge open plan room with a dining table set for twelve, three sofas and a TV, a small kitchen. Then five or six bedrooms with cubicles like you get in hospital with a curtain to pull across. In each one, there was a bed and a set of drawers. I wasn't staying here so I was safe, I thought, I was being punished. There were notices everywhere, rules and regulations, fire drills, mealtimes, rules for everything. What was this place and why were all these girls looking at me?

I was taken to another office – it was very cold, paperwork everywhere and again notices on the wall, a list of bedrooms one to twelve and someone's name in each box. I saw my name – cubicle 6. My eyes looking everywhere, my heart pounding from the stares I was getting off the other kids. All these strangers surrounding me, I was petrified and did what I do best – I just clammed up. I didn't want to speak to anyone. I knew I was in enough trouble already – why else had they put me in here? Why had I opened my big mouth? I thought I would get to stay with Emma. At least I thought her mum and dad would take me in – they were so nice to me.

They started asking me lots of questions, but here I was in this freezing cold office with rules and regulations and my name on cubicle 6. Now I was a number on a board, I wanted to go home. I had smelly Francis and this stern-looking Scottish woman with glasses and a chain around her neck holding them in place, she was a well-built lady with flowery elasticated skirts and a jumper. She frightened me if she smiled, I was sure her face would crack. Her name was Mavis, who I soon found out was called Battleaxe by all the other kids. I watched the film Matilda years later and headmistress Trunchbull was Mavis. The look, the walk, the face. If she smiled, I'm sure she would have fallen to pieces, she would have smashed. I just wished I could have been Matilda and had a happy ending. So, the attitude began – I refused to speak, just sat there whilst these two horrendous women were asking me questions and my mask was on full display. Question after question I would just smile, I was mute.

After an hour of being in the office and not saying a word, they took me to my bedroom, sorry cubicle, yes cubicle 6 was one of the square spaces that you pulled a curtain across. No door no privacy, no locks, a small square with a bed and dressing table and an itchy blanket and bars on the windows. I didn't have any clothes or belongings, so I pulled my curtain across and just sat there. Staring out the window. Mavis came back – "Emma, you have a visitor," she said. I was so pleased they took me through the experience of the doors again, unlocking and locking every door. As we went through, I knew it was going to be my mum. She had come to get me, she would have sorted it all out, even if she didn't like me. I was still her child and what would people think of her, if I was in a place like this. Yes, it would be my mum and she was going to cuddle me and pretend that she was sorry that all this had happened, and she was going to cry and love me.

I walked through the doors smiling. "Sit down on this sofa," said Battleaxe, "I'll go get your visitors." Visitors? Maybe it was Mum and Craig and it was all going to be over. The door opened and in walked Emma with her parents. Even better I thought, I ran over and gave them a hug – I was so pleased to see them. "We're only allowed ten minutes," she said, "we have brought you some toiletries and PJs." Emma then gave me a teddy bear with best friends on. "Why aren't you allowed to take me or even stay?" I asked them. "You still have a lot of talking to do with the police lady, and you will have to sleep here tonight but we will be here to see you tomorrow, to see what is happening." I was gutted but Mavis was there the whole time and she wasn't getting to see me emotional. "OK," I said, "I'm sure I'll be OK until tomorrow."

I never saw Emma or her mum and dad again. I never had chance to thank them for saving me. I never explained how they made me feel when I was at their house. I never had the chance to tell them how special they made me feel, that I actually felt a part of a family for a short while. A lot of years have gone by, but I can still see their faces clear as day. They helped me so much and that one day when I thought I was getting into trouble – the day Emma's mother rang the police actually saved me from so much more heartache and abuse that I would have received at home. In fact, I did see Emma a few times, many years later, but it was a bit awkward between us. By this point we were older and knew exactly what had happened to me, we knew it was awkward to talk about what had happened. At the end of the day, it was her mum that put me in a care home where I spent the next four years, isolated from everyone but I thank her for that. God knows how much more I would have endured, they protected me and as much as I wish they could have loved me and nurtured me, my bitch of a mother wanted to cut me off from everyone and she did.

After they had gone that day, I went back to my cubicle. I could hear all the other kids talking – one of them said, "Well she's not saying much and she's not a crier, we will see what she's like at dinner time." I never made dinner or supper, the police never came back that night, so I just sat on my bed staring out the window holding my new teddy bear. I slept for a couple of hours and in the morning, I could hear a lot of commotion, everyone getting ready for school. "Emma, come on, breakfast." I just stayed where I was. After all the shouting and banging had finished, the place went silent. Has everyone gone, I thought, I must be on my own. I wanted to explore where I was actually living. I peeped my head out the curtain and looked both ways – everything looked the same, every curtain was the same colour, every bed had the same duvets and the same thin, trodden carpets. I went into the tiny kitchen. I was hungry – I'd not eaten since I got there. I opened the fridge – surprise, surprise – everything had a label on it in there as well. I picked up a yoghurt and was just about to open it. "Put that back, this instance, mealtimes are very strict and you have missed breakfast, you now have to wait for lunch. Have you made your bed?" I just shook my head. "Well, you do not leave your cubicle until your bed is made and you do not come to the table in your pyjamas! You will be washed and dressed. Now go and get dressed and make your bed." "But I haven't got any clean clothes," I said. "Put your dirty ones back on, you will be OK for now." I went into my cubicle, eyes filled with tears, but I was angry. What a bitch that woman was, and this was supposed to be a care home. I thought, there is nothing caring about her at all, she is a dragon.

There was no TV in your room or music. It was a very lonely space, even for me who spent a lot of time locked in my room at home but at least I had my dolls to play with there. I went into one of the many bathrooms to have a wash, read all of the notices on yet another notice board then just went and sat back on my bed. There was a big field surrounding the place but nothing pretty about it, it had burnt grass, brown in places, no flowers or fruit trees just a big open boring space, but even so, I hoped I could go out there. It might have made me feel calmer and safe as the outdoors always had. When the police arrived that day, I was down. I didn't want to talk to them. I didn't want to talk to anyone, so I didn't. They were asking me questions and I just remained silent, not showing any emotion. The only thing I said was where's my mum and Emma and her parents. The police told me that they had spoken to my mum and she had given them some clothes for me because I was underage. 11 is classed as a minor – imagine being told you were a child when I felt like a woman in a baby's body. I had probably had more sex than any of them sat there and definitely more than Mavis. Maybe that was what was wrong with her. If she had had a bit of loving in the bedroom, she might have smiled more. So I was a minor and although I was under the care of social services until I was 18 – I had been placed on the child protection register – my bitch of a mother still had parental say over me and she had told the care home that I wasn't allowed any visitors other than her and my sister. So, it was her that stopped Emma and her family from coming to see me. It was her that put me in what turned out to be basically solitary confinement, sat in my cubicle day after day with no one allowed to see me.

Every day I was there I was getting darker and darker and angrier and angrier and I was there for four years. My mum came to a few meetings but that was it and I saw my sisters once. Apparently, my sisters didn't like seeing me in there. I remember the time my eldest sister came with her boyfriend – "What have you done?" she said, "why are you saying all this stuff, why are you being so evil?" I just looked at her – what was I saying wrong? I was telling the truth. I never saw her there again – it's the only time she ever came to visit me. It wasn't until I was in my thirties – imagine all that time in care, being a recluse, your whole family turned against you, aunties, uncles. No one spoke to me – my mother had poisoned them all against me, turned my whole family against me when I was 11 years old and still wouldn't let me have any visitors.

My sister Sharon came to see me years later. I was living in a caravan at the time with my four children – I'd just found out my husband was having an affair. It was another bit of trauma to add to the ongoing shit in my life. At the time, I couldn't even believe I'd made it to my thirties, and then after her shunning me in care, acting disappointed in front of her boyfriend, probably slagging me off and calling me the problem child, she decided twenty-three years later to tell me that Craig had tried it with her but she was older and told him to fuck off. I asked her why she didn't tell Mum or why when I was left to rot in care that she had never spoken up for me and she told me she never said anything because she didn't want to hurt Mum. Hurt fucking Mum, the woman deserves hurting, she chose a paedophile over her child. She married him after leaving me in care and they're still together to this day. I sat there as she told me all this – the disappointment running through me. She could have stopped all this, she could have helped me all those years ago. I wouldn't have had to go through everything I did – but she didn't want to hurt Mum. That night she apologised and told me if I wanted her to, she would go to the police and make a statement.

I rang the police instantly. I had a glimmer of hope that for the first time he was going to get locked up, I spoke to them in-depth, went through everything once more, all the hurt and pain coming back to me, but I was happy of course. I was angry at my sister for never saying anything before, but happy she finally had. The police went around to my mother's house once again. I remember sitting there thinking after all this time he's not going to be expecting this, he's going to get screwed.

Waiting for the police to get back to me was tiring. I couldn't sleep or settle. I was planning my celebration, finally feeling some pleasure in what they had put me through and what I had put myself through emotionally – numerous suicide attempts, bulimia, self-harming that is how I dragged myself up. It was the only control I had, hurting myself. I had to have some control of something, my mother was controlling my childhood. The care home was controlling my every move and the only thing I could control was my inner self. They couldn't make me eat, they couldn't stop me from hurting myself, they couldn't control what drugs or alcohol I was pumping inside me. It was my escape. Cutting myself used to make me feel good. It hurt but I'd smile. I'd sit cutting my legs and face to pieces and smile because it was me doing it, and it was making me control my emotions. If I could hurt myself like this and not shed a tear how was anyone else going to hurt me? They couldn't.

I have stopped the self-harming as an adult but still struggle with the bulimia. When I'm happy I'm OK, but it's when I can't cope with things. I control it better though now. I control what I eat and I have a problem with my insides, they don't work together – my bowels, gall bladder and pancreas don't communicate and my body can't cope with any fats so it means I'm on the toilet a lot. It helps keep my weight down but I think I may have caused this from all the times I made myself sick to control my weight. The last time I cut myself was 18 years ago when I was at the height of my bulimic ways. That was when me and my husband split up – another trauma that I took out on my own body. The thought of him being with another woman was bad enough, but it was a younger girl and I just – what the hell was wrong with me? I hadn't been a bad wife. I did the best I could. I'm not a princess I don't ask for much, I'm independent, I've always worked to look after my family. I hadn't burdened him with any of my past. I've never told anyone the things I have had the courage to write here. I've never trusted anyone enough. I've always hidden my past and my emotions. I've always appeared strong – hard-faced even – so why would someone I had been with for so long want to speak to someone younger than himself?

I left anyway, ran away again and that was the end of us but once again as I did when I was growing up I took all my pain out on myself. I was 6 stone wearing children's clothes and one day I asked my eldest daughter, who would have been 11 or 12, a question. I was in the bathroom just looking at myself, hating who I was. I had cut my legs to pieces. I used to write things on myself to remind me how horrible I was. Write things like slag, whore or things like – no one loves you. That way I could sit and read them and I would have them engraved in my skin as a constant reminder. I would always cut myself in places no one could see. It wasn't for attention – I didn't want anyone seeing my pain but I could remind me of what I thought about myself. This particular day I was in a bad place. I'd made myself sick all morning. I stood there staring at myself and all I could see was fat not just fat, obese I was disgusting. No wonder everyone would be horrible to me. I completely believed everything that had happened to me was my own fault. I hated myself more every day when I looked at myself – I was repulsive. I turned to my daughter and asked her if I had a double chin. Yes, she said. She didn't even know what a double chin was and why would I ask her. I was in a very bad place, I locked the bathroom door took a razor blade and started slicing my face open, stroke after stroke, digging the razor into my face trying to squeeze out the fat from my chin. I didn't stop until you couldn't see anything on my face but blood. Then I just walked into my bedroom, got into bed and stayed there for three days.

I put my eldest through so much – I depended on her too much and that is something I will feel eternally guilty for. I blame myself for her problems – I lost my path as a mother for a while and that I believe had a massive effect on a child who was like my best friend before all of this. When I finally got out of bed, letting my children see my face, I told them I fell but my oldest wasn't stupid. I thought she would believe me but I know now she never believed me and seeing me like that must have had a devastating effect on her. That was the last time I cut myself standing there in the bathroom that day, trying to prize fat out of a skeleton body, wearing clothes age 10-12 years and feeling disgusting in my own skin. I was losing myself and I was better than that. I'd fought with myself for too long to let myself down this way – it had to stop there and then and it did.

When the police finally came back to me, they told me once more they were not going to pursue the matter any further, that they couldn't connect it to a case from years ago and that my case had been closed for too many years for them to investigate it. So once again there I was, slap in the face time. My only option was to just leave them to enjoy their lives in peace whilst I fight with mine every day. It's always the victim that suffers especially when no charges are brought. You're made to feel like a liar. Apparently, you're innocent until proven guilty – well I know from experience that is the biggest load of bullshit. I will stand by what that man did to me until the day I die and I was the one that was treated as the guilty party. I was the one that got put away. I'm the one that has to deal with everything by myself whilst everyone else cracks on with their lives. All I could do was bury it – bury everything deep inside me to stop it from destroying me. Being in there was the loneliest time of my life and it definitely made me go inwards on myself. I still can be that way – I overthink everything. I just get lost in a mash-up of thoughts I can't control. Once I start thinking about something it won't go away, whereas I used to bury things in my mind and forget about it, my brain won't do that anymore. Everything is just on the surface eating away at me until I have a solution for it, or until my mood changes. I am up and down I can be deliriously happy then boom I'm so sad. I guess that's the PTSD kicking in, but I can't use that. I have to take responsibility for myself. I have to think about others around me. They don't understand my emotional state, so I'll just keep wearing my mask.

Day after day in the care home I became more reclusive, spending time on my own just lying on my bed. I couldn't speak about anything, about how I felt being removed from home, about my new life in care. Everything was either a blank look or a smile. I had been in care just short of a week and the lady in charge of the Girls section came back. She had been away on holiday up till then. I'd met Mavis, a Welsh man who was actually OK and a young woman who I felt really sorry for towards the end of my time there. She tried too hard and the girls gave her a really hard time. The home was split into Girls and Boys section although you never got to see the boys. If you got sent for milk or bread from the canteen you might see them playing snooker but apart from that, it was totally separate.

I got called to the office to have a chat with the lady in charge. She can't be worse than Mavis I thought to myself. I walked into the room and there in front of me was this beautiful woman with long blonde hair and the most stunning, welcoming, warm smile. "Hey," she said. "I'm sorry I've not met you yet, come in and have a chat." We sat in the room for over an hour. She didn't ask me difficult questions so I instantly felt compassion towards her. She spoke to me about her holiday and asked me about me what music I liked. She was so different from the rest of the people there, happy and positive. I liked her instantly. I went to bed that night feeling more settled and relaxed.

I woke up the next morning and went for breakfast. She was there again – her name was Diane and once again, I was greeted by her warm smile. I told her my foot was hurting. It had been hurting since I fell in Wales. "Let's have a look," she said. I took off my sock – my foot was black. "How did you do that?" she asked. I explained to her what had happened when I ran away to Wales and she told me to get my coat and she was going to take me to the hospital. After an x-ray and a few hours wait, they told me I had broken my foot and couldn't believe I hadn't got it sorted sooner. How was I meant to get it sorted? I wouldn't speak to anyone before Diane came along. I ended up having my foot in plaster for almost six months. Every time they tried to take the plaster off, my foot would just fall to the side. I had walked on it that long whilst broken, I had caused a lot of damage.

I'd been in the care home for just over a week when Diane told me we were going to have a meeting the next day with her, Social Services, the police and my mother. My heart sank when she said my mother. I hadn't seen her since I got put in there. I'd tried to ring her, but she never answered. I hadn't been told anything, just day by day things like it takes time to sort all these things out and the police would be investigating, so to hear news of a meeting was exciting – it might be time for me to go home finally. I had not been to school, so no one knew what had happened to me. There were no mobile phones or internet, you were lucky to have a telephone in your house, so I didn't know anybody's phone number apart from my mum's and she wouldn't answer. The meeting was planned for 1pm on the Friday morning. Everything was going to be sorted – I hadn't spoken to any of the kids in the home. I'd say hello at mealtimes but then just go back to my room. It wasn't until Diane came that I started opening up a bit, but that was only with her. I went to bed that night thinking of what I was going to do at the weekend when I got home. I couldn't walk very far because of the plaster on my leg but thought about seeing Tabby and playing with my Sindy dolls. The following morning when I got up, I made my bed and got dressed. I didn't want any breakfast. I felt sick inside – I was nervous about seeing my mum. I knew she was going to shout at me because Craig told me this was going to happen. He said my mum wouldn't love me anymore if I told about what we did together, but he had to be wrong. It was my mum, she would be OK probably, just tell me not to do it again, like always.

At 12.45 pm Diane took me into the main building of the home and into this huge room with a long table surrounded by big chairs. Francis was the first to arrive in her tweed and farm jacket. She came and asked me if I was OK, then went out of the room with Diane leaving me sat there all alone. They were gone for ages and then walked in with the lovely policewoman but my mother was nowhere to be seen. They sat down, and all turned to me. This was that day I got the truth – the day that turned my world upside down. The policewoman proceeded to tell me about sexual abuse. She told me what had been going on with Craig was very wrong, that he was not allowed to touch me the way he did and that I could never go back home. I tried correcting her and told her he only did those things because I was special and that he looked after me, but they all shook their heads. What Craig had been doing to me was illegal and in the eyes of the law, he could go to prison. They explained in detail the rights and wrongs of looking after a child, they told me that my body should never have been touched and that I could never go home.

"Where is my mum?" I asked. Diane put her head down and sighed. "Sweetheart," she said, "your mum's not coming and unfortunately she doesn't believe you. She said nothing like that could ever happen in her house, she said that you're a naughty child who she can't control, she said you were never left on your own with Craig, she said you used to run away all the time and that since you started high school you've become a stranger to her."

She had also told them about me being in a coma and about me running away. The policewoman then told me that there wasn't enough evidence against Craig and that nothing was going to happen to him. "So why do I have to stay here, then?" I said. "For your own protection." I didn't understand. If what Craig had done to me didn't matter, why couldn't I go home? It did matter, they said, but they couldn't prove it. They then told me I was moving schools and they were going to try and find foster parents to look after me. It was so much to take in, I couldn't cope. Was Craig wrong? Why didn't my mother believe what I'd told the police? It wasn't a bad thing if he loved me. And why were these people telling me it was bad, but nothing was going to come from it? I asked if I could go back to my room. As I walked through the corridor, doors locking behind me, I knew this was where I was going to be for a while. I better make some friends, I thought.

Everything was going to be different now. I was starting a new school and waiting for new parents. Since my meeting I had stopped talking completely, I would just smile. Diane had one on ones with me almost every day, explaining sexual abuse until I fully understood what had happened.

All that did was make me hate myself more – in fact, that was the start of hating myself. No wonder my mum doesn't want anything to do with me, I thought. She must hate me, all the things I had done with her partner. I was ashamed of myself. I didn't want to be me anymore and I just changed. I became someone else overnight. My mum said I was a horrible child who was always naughty and that is what I was to become.

There was a smoking-room in the care home and that's where all the girls used to go to have a laugh and chat without any staff around, but you had to be 16 to smoke then or get permission off your parents. Of course, my mother wouldn't give me permission. She wouldn't answer the phone or come and see me but she refused to let me smoke. I had to get in that room – you never really knew anyone until you were in there. That's where you could laugh, that's where they talked about everyone including me because I couldn't be a part of it.

I tried forming bonds in the home with people but there were only two girls that made an impact on my life, one of them was a part-timer. She used to come in for a few days when her mum couldn't cope with her behaviour. Her brother spent a stint in there as well, but they were with me in my new school so I became very close to her. She only lived around the corner from the home so it was funny when she used to 'pop in' for the weekend as we would say. I'm sure she came just to have a catch up with us. And another girl who became my best friend, my confidant. We went to watch our first ever movie together at the pictures. It was so exciting – neither of us had been before. We went to watch La Bamba – I cried at the end, so she took the piss out of me for weeks of course. We got dropped off and picked up, but it was nice to have the time on our own.

I still felt like I was missing out on being in the smoking-room and with so many children coming and going, some would come for a day or a few weeks but it was only me and Tammy that were there the whole stint. She had been there a few months before I got there. She was very much like me, we would laugh and mess about, but I never told her why I was there and she never told me. I think that's why we got on so well – we were both someone else, too ashamed or afraid, to tell the truth. Too scared to be who we really were – vulnerable children. Her mask was as prominent as mine and while we could laugh our way through our time in there we would be OK. We never had one cross word in four years always stuck together.

My anger towards my mother was growing. I rang her every Sunday night but after a while, I stopped. I didn't need her – I had Tammy and she had me, but I came up with a plan to get in the smoking-room. I'd been there around four months and still not started school because of my leg being in plaster. I was being home schooled which was a complete waste of time because unless I was with Tammy I refused to speak to anyone still, apart from Diane but she was always so busy in meetings or on courses I didn't see her very much. Tammy was always in the smoking-room and I was stuck with Mavis. This had to change!

There was a door that went straight from the Girls' wing without going through the whole building and it was open for two half hours in the day – once in the morning for everyone to go to school and once in the evening when they were coming back. Tammy didn't go to a normal school – she went to a school for naughty kids. She would tell me about it, that they used to just play games and do puzzles all day. This sounded amazing – while I was in a room with a woman I wouldn't talk to. I'd just complete the work as fast as I could and get out of there.

Then, one day, I was sat on the sofa watching TV and Mavis opened the door ready for everyone coming home. She told me she was going to the canteen to get some milk and as soon as she went, I just walked out the door, well hobbled with my plaster on my leg. My heart was pounding. I got to each corner and popped my head around, then headed to the next, hoping not to be caught. I had escaped. I was in the open world once again but with only one thing in my mind – I was going to get in the smoking-room and I knew exactly how to do it.

My mother lived about 6 miles from the home and with no money or coat and a plaster on my leg that was a marathon for me, now 12 years old. I had spent my birthday with Tammy and Mavis – no cards or present from my family, but I didn't care. By that point, my hatred towards all of them was at its highest but I knew how to get what I wanted and that marathon walk was going to get me everything. By the time I got to my mum's, I was exhausted. I stood in the garages at the back of the house for a while just looking to see if I could see any movement in the house. I walked down the path picked up the bin and the key was there – no one was home. What a stroke of luck! I went in and went looking for Tabby but he wasn't there. I went to my room – it was empty, my toys had gone, my dolls' house, no bedding on my bed. It was like I'd never lived there.

I went back downstairs and into the posh room, turned the TV on and just sat there. I was hoping my plan would work but I was so frightened. I'm returning home to face the woman who's abandoned me, and I could possibly face the man who abused me and got away with it, I thought. By this point, I knew exactly what he had done, and I didn't know how I was going to be with Mum, let alone him. Mum came back first, luckily. What would he have done if he had been confronted by me? I heard her coughing, as usual and the sound of the kettle being put on. She came into the hallway to hang her coat up and there I was sat on the posh sofa. "What are you doing here?" she said. "I've run away, Mum, I can't stay there. It's horrible. Why have you left me there?" I carried on telling her about the rules and meal times and how I wasn't allowed out and I missed her and the place scared me. "You can't stay here," she said. "I can't stay there either," I replied. "It's horrible and you have the say on everything, Mum, you won't even let me go in the smoking-room and that's the only place I can get away from people and feel safe, you won't let anyone visit me and I'm on my own all the time. I can't go back, Mum, I can't go back there, please don't send me back."

As I was talking to her, the phone rang I could hear her – "Yes, she's here. OK, I'll keep her here till you get here." I stood up. "I'm going, Mum, you can't send me back there." Within a few minutes, there was a knock at the door. They can't be here that quick, I thought, but it was the police. They had to come to wait with me until someone arrived from the care home. The policeman sat with me in the posh room and my mum went in the other and shut the door. When the door went again, to my surprise, it was Diane. She had come to get me. She didn't say anything to me but asked to speak to my mum. She went in for a while and they came out together. "You can't come here," Diane said. "I thought you were OK, I thought you were settling down." I told her I wasn't happy I hated it there and I was staying with my mum. Mum said I couldn't and she looked stressed. She wanted me out before Craig got home, I knew it. "OK, I'll go," I said, "but can I have visitors and be allowed in the smoking-room." "Yes, I suppose so," she said. I smiled and give myself up. Well, that was easy. As I sat in the car on the way back I knew she only let me have those things as long as I stayed away from her.

I don't want to be anywhere near you, Mother, but I know now my time in care will be better. And you said it, in front of the manager. So as a 12-year-old, I was allowed to smoke with my mother's permission and I was allowed to have visitors. No one came anyway but I got my mum to change her mind – just for me to stay out the way. What a wonderful mother you are, I thought.

5:

The Good Years

After my antics of running away, I got punished. I was grounded for a month – no pocket money and no smoking. I'd gone through all that to be put on a smoking ban. I couldn't believe it, but me and Tammy found it hilarious. After being in care for six months I still had no visitors, but I was finally allowed to smoke! Me and Tammy spent that much time in there doing our own thing, our bond grew stronger. Diane called me into the office one day and told me I was to see a psychologist later that day. "What for?" I asked. "To assess your emotional state. Your emotions are starting to worry us – you don't show any."

"I'm fine," I said.

When I got called into the room a friendly-looking lady sat there. "Hello, Emma," she said, "it's nothing to worry about, we are just going to go through a few things." Now I know I was only twelve years old, but I wasn't stupid. There were around 8 pieces of A4 paper on the table in front of me. "Turn one over at a time," she said, "tell me what you see." I turned over the first piece of paper and there was a smiley face on it. "What do you see, Emma?" she asked. "A smiley face," I said. "Well done, Emma, well done." I sat there looking at her, was this woman for real? Was she seriously asking me what that was? "Now, onto the next one," she said. I turned over the next piece of paper. It was another face, but this time with gritted teeth and steam coming out of the ears. "Now what do you see?" "Angry," I said.

We continued this way until all the pieces of paper had been turned over – confused, sad, cold, hot. I told her what I saw on every piece of paper she showed me. "Well done, Emma, you got them all right." I just burst out laughing. "I'm sorry," I said, "but I'm twelve years old – I'm not a baby." "Then why don't you show any of these emotions in your day-to-day life? The only emotion you show is the smiley happy face you turned over first." Her face changed to a face of concern. "I am trying to see if you understand emotion. I don't want to make you feel stupid but hiding behind your smile every day is starting to cause everybody around you to be concerned, do you understand what I'm saying, Emma?" "I understand," I said.

She told me I had to start talking to someone about how I felt, and it was very bad for me to keep storing things in my mind. I wish I had listened to her back then, but I thought I knew better – I had to take care of myself. The staff at the care home had enough to do with all the different mix of children in there. I was OK – they didn't need to worry about me as well. But I agreed to try and talk more, and she arranged to come and see me every week. I only saw her another two times. She gave up on me. I didn't know her – she was a stranger and she didn't make me feel comfortable. I didn't want her to know how I felt because apart from anger towards my mum and getting that what Craig had been doing was wrong, I tried to push it to the back of my head. I didn't want to be dealing with that, I wanted to forget it. I didn't want to think about it – why would I? It made me feel horrible and I had enough to deal with surviving in the home.

It was finally the day to take off the plaster that had dragged me down for six months, which meant it was time for me to start my new school. Starting a new school was hard enough, but starting in the middle of the second year, halfway through term, when people had already made their bonds and all the groups of different kids had been formed? How were people going to take to me? Did they have to know I was in a children's home? Were they going to judge me straight away? Kids can be cruel and I wasn't naughty, I was a mixed-up girl who had a smile on my face all the time, so no one could see what was inside me. So as long as I was just that person, pretend me, with no drama, surely people would like me.

I went to get my uniform with Diane. "I need to nip home," she said. She lived with her son – I didn't mind us nipping to her house, I could see where she lived. It was 15-20 miles from the care home on an estate of new houses – a really nice area. We got out the car and she let us into her house. Her son wasn't there. "Do you want a cup of tea?" "Yes please." We sat in her home, talking and it just came out of my mouth. "Will you be my new mum?" I asked her, "will you adopt me? You are so nice to me, you could look after me. I love you so much and I'd love you as my family." Diane's eyes filled with tears. "I'm so sorry, Emma, I can't be your new Mum."

She told me how hard her job was, how she couldn't get emotionally involved with the children she was working with. I still wanted to be loved so much and I was clutching at straws – anyone that showed an ounce of interest in me. But by putting myself out there, letting my guard down and showing some love and emotion, I was let down. I understand now, but I didn't at the time. I always thought I was her favourite and she was nicer to me than anyone else but maybe I just wanted to believe that. I didn't speak to her all the way home. In fact, I didn't speak to her very much again. Why should I speak to someone who I thought cared for me but was, in fact, just doing her job, and although she was very good at it, I was just a number. Her job was to make people feel loved and safe, but it wasn't to get attached or to form deep relationships with them and that hurt me.

When it came to my first day of starting school, I was allowed to walk on my own with strict instructions to come straight home when school finished. As I walked up the street to the school, I could feel all eyes on me. Nervously, I walked through the gates and made my way to the main office, explained who I was and was told to sit. A man with a bald head came out. "Come on, then, Emma, let's get you settled, your first lesson is PE." "I haven't got any PE kit," I said, hoping I could get out of it. "It's OK, we have spares!!!"

I was devastated. Since I had started to understand the way I had behaved when I was younger and the feelings and thoughts I felt towards my previous PE teacher, I didn't want to get undressed in front of anyone, ever again, and I definitely didn't want to wear a spare uniform on my first day of my new school. "Can I not just sit out of this one, Sir?" I asked. "No, Emma, physical education is very important." I walked up the stairs to the changing rooms to a row of stares from all the other girls. I smiled and carried on walking, I got introduced to our PE teacher and she was told I didn't have any kit. She went into her office and came out with some old PE uniform and scruffy trainers and handed them to me in front of everyone. I could hear them sniggering already and my back was up. I got undressed in the corner and there was a group of girls staring at me. "That's her," I heard one of them say, "the new girl from the children's home." They knew already who I was and I'd already been judged. I'd been there 10 minutes and I was the kid from the children's home, not Emma! I wanted to shout, my name's Emma and I'm nice and I'm scared, but I couldn't do that I would look weak.

We went outside and played hockey – my least favourite sport and I was nervous but couldn't show it. That hour I had a hockey stick smacked on my ankles 20 times. I wanted to cry but just smiled each time they hit me with it. We went back to the changing rooms and had to shower. I had no toiletries, so just stood in the shower for a few minutes before I realised I didn't have a towel. The PE teacher was nowhere to be seen, so I walked out of the shower naked, walked through the changing rooms and started to dry myself with my school jumper. Everyone was laughing at me – why send a girl into school and allow them to face this on their first day? I could feel the anger boiling through my body, I turned around and there was a girl stood there with ginger hair. "Simone wants to fight you at break." "Does she? Well, tell her to come ask me herself."

I turned around and carried on getting dressed, my legs shaking with fear. Next thing I could feel this hand on my hair, dragging me to the floor. "Don't for one minute think you will be coming into this school and thinking your hard, you tramp," she was shouting at me. I don't know where my strength came from but I just grabbed her hair back and threw her on the floor, jumped on top of her and started hitting her in the face. "Who's a tramp, I'll show you tramp!" I was screaming. Next thing, I was getting dragged off her and summoned to the headmaster's office. I sat there and he told me that he was not having my sort coming into his school and causing trouble. "But Sir, I haven't done anything – it was Simone that started it." "I'm not interested," he said, "Simone is a good student, I suggest if you want to fit in here, you change your ways immediately." Oh, I will, don't worry, I thought. I was judged immediately not only by the kids but by the teachers and headmaster. This wasn't going to go well and I wasn't about to be walked all over. You think I'm in a children's home because I'm naughty, you're so wrong but you will never know who I am. If you want naughty, that's what you're having.

My first day went from bad to worse. The fight I had at first lesson with Simone was a bad mistake – she was the head of one of the many groups that you have in school. This group was the naughty girls and I'd just dented that with my antics in PE I called it sticking up for myself, defending my corner but by the time I walked out of the school gates that day, I didn't have one friend. Everyone hated me. As I walked back to the care home, I was imagining going home to a nice family a warm house that smelt of home. Is there a smell that defines home? I think so, I still do it now. I walk into my home and need to smell that smell – it's safe. My home smells of protection which is difficult to explain, but it does. I walk in and feel immediately safe.

The walk home from school was a pretty one. There were big trees either side of the road and some beautiful houses. I loved that walk, didn't like where it led to, either school or the home, but my imagination took me elsewhere for twenty minutes. In the middle of all the houses, there was another school, a private school, but it fitted in with all its splendour and grandness. Nothing like my school. Every day I walked past, I would wonder what it would be like to go to that school. That was a school where privileged children went – the ones that were looked after and were clever. I didn't fit into any of those brackets. I was hated and stupid. I wasn't taught anything by my parents as I was growing up. Actually, that's not true, I was taught how to have sex and how to use a microwave. Oh, and how to keep your mouth shut.

As I got nearer home that day I was thinking about PE and was angry with the home for not sending me with a PE kit. It's all their fault, I thought, if I hadn't looked like a tramp and if I didn't have to dry myself with my jumper, maybe they would have left me alone. Or if I wasn't in the horrible place in the first instance people might have given me a chance. Instead I was hated by everyone, looked down on and becoming all the things they believed I was in one short 6-hour day. Nice one, Emma, made a great impression. As if my day wasn't bad enough I walked into Mavis, stern face, arms crossed, glaring at me. "Office now!" she said. Here we go, I thought, school have been on the phone. I'm in deep shit.

I sat down and off she went. Her angry face telling me what a let – down I was. How the school were good to take me. How I was portraying the care home to be a bad place and I'd let everybody down. I just sat there and let her go on. I could feel every lash of her vicious tongue swiping at me and I just smiled, apologised and went to my cubicle and got my pen and paper that they had given me to write my feelings on. I opened it up and wrote across one side of the paper my feelings. FUCK OFF – that's all I wrote. Those two words summed up how I felt. They weren't interested in me trying to fit in. They weren't interested that I was attacked first, that I was afraid, that I had no towel, that I had no uniform and that I'd spent the day getting hatred from every set of eyes that looked at me. Fuck off – that's all they deserved. I put my paper outside my cubicle and shut the curtains. Even the place I'm staying, I thought, the place that's meant to make me feel safe, the place that knows about me and is here to help me, well, even that place has you all figured out. They treat you exactly the same way everybody else does – like you're a piece of shit. Every one of them helped to create the monster that was the outside of me and not one of them knew me. I didn't go for dinner that night or supper, I just sat on my bed the whole time, worrying about the next day.

I was up washed and dressed by six-thirty, waiting for someone to shout at me. You weren't allowed in the living space until you were told to go in there. It was locked at night time – that way you couldn't use the smoking-room or raid the fridge, if you were hungry. We got called through for breakfast. Diane was there. "You want to talk about yesterday?" she said. "No, I don't, doesn't matter how it went anyway, you're not interested," I said. "I want to know how school was and what made you get so angry." I looked at her and wanted to cry but the other kids came in for breakfast. "We will talk later," she said. I nodded.

When I got to school, I felt like I had walked into a different place. Everyone I walked past said Hi or smiled at me. I walked into my class confused to be once again greeted with smiles. "Come and sit by us," one girl said. Have they got me mistaken with someone else, I thought. After registration, I went to my first lesson and Simone was there. She started walking towards me, my knees started shaking. "Can we have a truce?" she said, "I'm sorry for the way I treated you yesterday, come sit by me." It was over but now I was part of the group again – the group I needed in my old school, but did I want to be involved in this again? At least I was going to have some friends, I thought.

I just accepted my new situation. I wasn't at the school that long, I was asked to leave on my 14th birthday. By that point, I wasn't allowed in any lessons. I just typed all day, I wasn't naughty but I was disruptive. I just wanted to have a laugh, I didn't learn very much and wasn't able to take any exams, so there was no point doing my final year. The year and a half I was there, I made some good friends. I wasn't doing the things I'd done in the old school. I was just enjoying myself doing normal things, going around to friends' houses listening to music, going to the park. I had to be in for 7pm so I never had the chance to get involved in anything the other kids did. I wasn't drinking or stealing and there wasn't a penis in sight. It was the best year and half of my life. I was writing every night in my diary, getting things off my chest. Still sometimes writing fuck you or leave me alone on days when I felt down, but the majority of the time I would write other stuff which made me feel better. I was coming to understand the abuse I had gone through and trying to come to terms with the fact that my mother didn't give a shit.

By the time I was asked to leave school, I'd still not seen my mother. I had tried to ring her every Sunday but she never answered. I saw my eldest sister a couple of times and she had asked me to be bridesmaid at her upcoming wedding. I agreed, but was very anxious at the thought of not only seeing my mum but the whole family. None of them had spoken to me since I got taken away so it was very daunting for me. How were they going to treat me? But more importantly, I was going to come face to face with Craig, only this time I knew exactly who I was dealing with. I was coming face to face with the man who stripped me of my childhood, the man that completely ruined my life. And the man I now knew was a paedophile. Craig wasn't charged with anything, but I was on the child protection register until I was 18 and he was put on the sex offenders' register. Why put him on that if they didn't think he had done anything? I don't understand the justice system, I never have. That's their way of saying he is a paedo without charging him, what's all that about?

I used to listen to the Supertramp logical song when I was in care. It reminded me of myself – the line "they sent me away to teach me how to be sensible". I have my faults as we all do, but they did teach me how to be sensible and I was safe. I understand that now. My life changed. They give me back my childhood for a few years. I have slipped backwards and forwards throughout my life sometimes going back to the old me, not respecting myself. I've let people treat me badly to make them happy and I still find it difficult believing I'm worthy of things and of being loved. When this is complete and if it gets read, who's going to want to be with me. That's my worry –

who wants someone like me? I've never talked about this. Will my partner accept me? Who knows? That's another bridge I have to cross but I need to do this. I've needed to do this for a very long time and my breakdown helped, opening Pandora's box has released so many demons in my head and I have to face them now full-on. I can't pretend to be someone else anymore. I have to put myself out there – I have to expose not only him, but myself too. Maybe then I can start accepting who I am.

I'm still weak and I'm very vulnerable but I hide it quite well. Until I've consumed too much alcohol. If I've got things in my head and I drink, then it all comes out but in the wrong way. I hurt people that care about me instead of talking about what's in my head. Or I'll ask a question and won't believe the answer. I need to know I'm loved and if my head isn't in the right place, I won't believe it. Then it grows inside me until I explode over something that isn't even the issue in the first place. My psychiatrist said I cover things up. I want people to see the good in me all the time and I don't talk enough, but the trouble is I don't tell people about me, so how can they know when something's up. I have a bad day and you can see it in my face, but I keep closed off. So, I can make people insecure and believe they have done something to upset me or that I'm not interested in them.

Sometimes I just want to curl up in a ball and cry and for someone to hold me and just let me get through it but because I'm so shit at showing things I just look moody. Oh, she's on one again. I can't handle some situations but don't say anything – just put myself in a position where I'm listening or having a conversation about things I really don't want to talk about. Anything to do with paedophiles gives me flashbacks and unfortunately, we live in a society where it's rife and people talk about it all the time. They don't know how I feel about it, they don't see what I do when they're talking about it. They are angry that there are people out there like that, they don't see me re-living it, whilst they're talking about it. And I'm SO angry but if I were to try to talk about things like that in a conversation, I would get angry and emotional and then people would know my weaknesses and use it against me. I hate the way I feel, I shouldn't think that people will treat you badly but unfortunately, they did and they do. I have not had one relationship that hasn't had some kind of mistreatment whether it's been cheating or physical abuse or rejection. To trust someone and believe in someone is a hard task for me.

Because I wasn't in school I had to get a job – orders of the home. I started working weekends in a coffee shop and I was good at it. I started by waiting on, but within a few weeks, I was in the kitchen too, making sandwiches and microwave meals. I loved that job – it was for a company called P&A Davies – I don't think they're going anymore. They had a takeaway shop next door but one to the café and I did a few shifts in there too, even though I couldn't work full time until I left school. I was able to work all the school holidays so I was earning well for a 15-year-old and I still got my pocket money from care too.

If I wasn't at work I'd be writing in my ever-growing diary. I would write and leave it outside my cubicle and they would read it and put it back. We never spoke about what I'd written. In the latter days, it was just my way of releasing and I could pretend it was just my private thoughts and they could see how I was doing. By the time I left the care home, my diary was huge – page upon page of raw emotion. I would have liked to have kept it and I did for a few years. It was so personal to me – I caught one of my husbands reading it one day – yes one of my husbands – there have been two. Two unsuccessful attempts at loving and commitment, two unsuccessful attempts at letting anyone get close to me and trying to make me believe in them – more importantly for me to believe in myself. Failed.

Not just my marriages, every relationship. I've tried to have the same thing over and over. I give too much and am too soft and they take advantage, then I cannot forgive them, and I don't believe in them. As soon as I don't believe in someone, I'm gone, no questions asked, no room to talk. It's in my head – you're letting me down and you're going to hurt me and once that is there, I'm over them. No tears, no drama, I'm gone. It has been a constant battle throughout my adult life, trying to believe in someone I want to, and I do try so hard, but I have issues with men. I just don't trust them. I doubt why they're being nice to me. What do they want from me? When are they leaving or cheating or going to demand dirty things from me? It eats away at me constantly.

Maybe one day I will write about my life after care – that would be a lot bigger than this. I just seem to either attract the wrong people or not let the right people in. I am definitely what you call a dating fuck-up I think, until the relationship that I wrote about at the beginning of this book. He was a stranger – before him, I only ever dated people I knew. They thought they knew me so I didn't have to go into detail about anything or even mention any of this. I could keep hiding away, I guess. I have just had a realisation – it's only taken me 46 years. None of my relationships has worked because I never told anyone the truth. I see myself in an ugly light – a dirty horrible whore who had sex with animals and spastics. I never let anyone in my head, I never let anyone see the real me. Maybe now they might understand why I had no belief in them, maybe they might understand why I behaved the way I did, maybe one day they will forgive me too. And maybe even one day, I will try and forgive myself.

So, my endless relationship battles – two husbands and a few serious relationships, one of them was over 28 years on and off, since I was 18. My God, I don't know how many times we tried to make it work and there were definitely times I wanted it to work but at some point, I lost faith in him. I didn't believe a word and like I said, when I lose faith, I'm a goner. I tried with him the hardest that I've tried with anyone. I actually wanted him to touch me. I believed him when he held me, I longed for him to love me. The years had bonded us, I was the first person he had slept with. I still remember our first time all those years ago. He was 16 and I was 18. He used to come around to my flat and I fancied his best friend – his friend was good-looking with lovely hair, very quiet and quite shy. He was called Louis and the guy I ended up with was Mat. Louis asked Mat if he should get involved with me and Mat told him no chance. He put him off me, said my last boyfriend was a nutcase and that he would hit him if he got involved with me. That wouldn't have happened – my last boyfriend wasn't bothered about what I did. His girlfriend was though, she smashed me over the head with a baseball bat – straight in the face, actually. He wasn't bothered about that, either. So anyway, Matt put Louis off me, because he had intentions of his own. We have laughed about that in the past. We started sleeping together but it had to be a secret. Mat's choice – he said he felt bad for Louis because of his lies to him. We were seeing each other in secret for a while and I said it had to stop – we either come out or it's done, so he said we were done. I didn't see him for a while then one night he knocked on my door. I let him in, but I was dating someone else by then I could see the upset in his eyes. The next time I saw him, I was 8 months pregnant and married. He walked past me at the bus stop, saw my pregnant state, shook his head and told me I was making the worst mistake of my life.

Roll on 7 years and a drug-fuelled night out in Liverpool and who do I bump into but Mat? We stopped and talked for a long time. By this point, I had four children and had split up from the second husband. I was living in Wales. We swapped numbers and said we would keep in touch. The next day we turned into text warriors, none stop messaging each other. It was great – he came up to see me in Wales and we started once again. He told me he would never fall in love with me and I bet him he would. I thought I was so in love – I actually felt my heart pound when he came near me. No one had ever made me feel like that. We were having a good time and I shared with him probably the best Valentine's day I'd ever had, and will ever have. It is a great memory.

The day after Valentine's day, he was going on holiday with his friends. I missed him when he was gone. I never spoke to him whilst he was away. When he came back he bought me a bottle of Dior – *Forever and Ever*. I'd never smelt it before and it was beautiful. You can only buy it from airports now in the duty-free shop and I have bought myself a few bottles over the years, always reminds me of Mat. When he gave me the perfume he told me not to read anything into the name of it – *Forever and Ever*. Turns out we spent most of my life trying to make it forever and ever, so the name definitely meant something ironically. After us seeing each other for eight or nine months I found out he had a girlfriend and he lived with her. She didn't know anything about me and I didn't know anything about her. I ended it instantly. Was I upset? Yes – but it was a way of life for me, it was normal by that point to be lied to and cheated on and rejected. He had a phone with dual SIM cards and would switch them over when he spoke to me. Very clever – I had never heard of anything like that back then.

We didn't speak for a while then when we got in touch again, he told me they had separated – she had found out about another girl he was seeing whilst he was seeing me too. The thing with Mat was that when he was younger, he was a bit scruffy and didn't have very much but he made himself into someone quite successful and turned into a very handsome man. I think that got to him a bit and he thought he could have what he wanted. Anyway, we decided to try again – he promised this time would be different. We were in a good place, happy, but he still hid things from me. He would always walk in a place before me and look around to see if he knew anyone, always walk a few steps ahead of me and we never went out in his local area always miles away. I didn't find it suspicious at first, I should have, but we were having a good time, so I just let it go over my head – one more time of me wanting to live in my fantasy world. There was a point with Mat where I would have done anything for him and I proved that and destroyed my own soul in the process!

I had four children and had to have a hysterectomy when I was very young because of endometriosis and cancerous cells on my ovaries, so they took everything away in my early twenties. He didn't have any children and he longed for one of his own. So, thinking I was doing the right thing I agreed he could continue his relationship with the other woman he was seeing behind his ex-girlfriend's back. Yes, the dinners in the country and the walking in front of me and checking who was in a venue before we could sit down was because he was still seeing this woman. But like I said, I would have done anything for him, so he continued with her, staying over, having sex, pretending he was in a relationship with her basically, but I knew about it. She never knew I existed and to him because I was involved and I knew his intentions, he wasn't cheating, and it was OK for him to go and have another life with another woman.

He rang me one day and said he needed to speak with me. He came and picked me up and we went for a drive. He told me in the car that she was pregnant, and he was going to continue the relationship until the baby was born and even go and stay with her for a few weeks, so he could bond with his child. I told him I was happy for him. This was what he had always wanted, and I couldn't give him a child, so I was sure I was doing the right thing. Every night he spent there, I couldn't sleep. I had vivid pictures in my head of them making love, I could see him touching her and I could hear him whispering things in her ear, hear him telling her he loved her. I felt sick but when I saw him I pretended I was OK. I stuck with him the whole pregnancy and when she gave birth and he moved in with her for a while to bond with the baby, I still stayed.

He showed me a picture of his little girl – she was his pride and joy and still is to this day. I had her picture engraved on a glass figurine for him for his birthday. I hadn't met his daughter because the other woman lived 40 miles away from me – pretty easy to lead two separate lives. By the time I did get to meet his daughter she was a few months old. I couldn't look at her and I'm ashamed to admit it, but the hatred I felt. The pain I had put myself through for him to be happy. I had so much anger towards this little baby and even more towards him. I had to go. I couldn't be in this relationship anymore. What had I done to myself? Why did I put myself through that, trying to please someone else, trying to make them happy?

Well I did and he was happy, and I was a woman with no self-worth. Three more times we have tried, and I can honestly say – I know deep in the bottom of my heart – the last three times we tried, he loved me, worshipped the ground I walked on, but I was already on the road to a massive breakdown. Knowing the man you love is fucking another woman and yes, what he got in the end was worth it, but it destroyed me. He would have done anything to prove to me how much he loved me. He would have, I know that, but my feeling towards him, the way I felt cheated. I couldn't believe a word he said. I doubted him all the time and now we don't speak. The last time we did, I told him about my writing and said that if he ever got the chance to read it, he might understand where I went, how we lost each other. But I could hear the hatred in his voice. I broke his heart – I never meant to, but I did, but I didn't have a heart to give. It had been buried deep inside me. I know he will do OK – he will fall in love with someone else, maybe have more children, who knows? But I know he will be OK, and I made peace with his daughter. Over the years, I grew to love her – she's a beautiful young lady now and, in his eyes, and eventually mine, she was worth it.

After finding someone reading my diary, I was mortified. They were my deepest, darkest thoughts that I never wanted to share with anyone. No one had a right to even open it without my permission and to see someone holding it, looking over the last 16 years of my life, I took it and burned it. To date, the biggest mistake I have ever made. And there's been a few. I wish I still had those thoughts and feelings, when I locked everything away for so long. Maybe I wouldn't have, if I had that to reflect on, maybe I would have kept writing and healing myself along the way. I don't remember anything I wrote in that diary apart from fuck off and fuck you and leave me alone. I can see it in big red pen, but I wish I could see how I felt back then. I wish so much I still had that diary. It was a part of me – my whole life was in there. Well, I definitely cannot get it back and I hid so much for so long. I guess I want to know if I have grown, if I have let go of some things, if the same things still bother me now that bothered me then. I want to know the feelings I had towards my mother instead of the anger I feel now.

I remember ringing her and crying, I remember needing my mother on many occasions throughout my life. I wonder if she ever thinks about me. I remember her birthday being March 15. I think about her a lot. I am scared for when she passes away, I still live in hope that she will answer my questions. I would like to think she would explain why she did what she did, why she let this happen to me? Not just when I was younger but my whole life. How can someone love me when my own mother doesn't? Why did she turn her back on me? And when she's gone, how am I going to feel? Will I be upset? Will I be angry? Or will I finally feel some peace because I can't know anymore how she felt about me?

I don't know how old she is – I'm guessing in her seventies, so my time wondering all of these things is running out. I guess that's another bridge to cross when the time comes. I did ring her when my granddaughter was born. I told her she was a great grandmother and asked if she would like to meet to see her and she just said no and put the phone down. And changed her number. I don't have the same anger towards my father, as I do my mother. I wanted to write about my father but there's really not much to say. I'm friends with him on Facebook but I'm not allowed to contact him because his wife won't like it. I've seen him maybe 4 times in my life maybe 5, he lives in Scotland. I have met his brother he used to drink in a pub I worked in years ago. He never treated me like his niece – he was just a punter – he never knew I grew up in care. My father knows nothing about me. He wouldn't be able to tell you when my birthday is. I added my sisters on Facebook – the two girls he had with his new wife – but they never spoke to me, so I deleted them. The last time I saw my dad he had been arguing with his wife and had to get away, so he turned up on my doorstep, got pissed, told me what a bad father he had been, apologised and left. I sent him a message on Father's Day 2017 saying Happy Father's Day I love you, but he never replied. Stupid of me sending it really, I don't love him I have no clue who the man is. He's a stranger. He said his new family don't understand why I want to be in touch and his wife won't accept him talking to me, so he doesn't want to upset them.

Got to laugh, OK, Daddy, no worries. I'll just stay out the way, as long as your new family are OK. Don't be worrying about me.

Where Next?

It was coming up to the time where we were talking about where I would go when I left care. My oldest sister, whose wedding was coming up very soon, said I could go and live with her, but once again my mother still had parental control over me till I was 18 and she fought with my sister and said I wasn't allowed to go there. I had nowhere to go. Tammy was moving out too, she was going a few months before me and they had arranged for her to go to a hostel not too far from the care home, so that was an option for me. I was starting to feel scared going out to the big wide world on my own at 16 and I had my sister's wedding coming up which was terrifying me. That wedding scared me so much that I don't remember it. I don't remember being there and if I hadn't seen pictures, I would have questioned that I was there. I completely blocked everything out of my head. Even now I try and remember but all I see is the steps at the back of the church and me standing on them. In the pictures, my sister looked beautiful and I looked well after four meals a day in care – it certainly didn't help my waistline. I don't remember the evening reception or the wedding breakfast. I'm wondering if I went to them or if I just went to the church but the whole day is a complete blank. I don't know if my mother spoke to me, I don't know if Craig was there.

I find it so strange that the whole day is blocked from my memory. However, my psychiatrist did say that now I've started letting things out, everything will come out eventually but my traffic queue of memories, hidden for all this time, is going to take a while for my brain to process. So hopefully one day I will remember. I don't want to hide everything away, not one detail. I need to remember everything, so I can deal with things and only when I have dealt with everything will I be able to put all this behind me and cope with things better and who knows maybe let someone love me – that would be good.

My oldest sister Sharon asked me to go for dinner one night in her new home. I asked the care home and they agreed and lifted my usual 7pm curfew to 9.30 the first time in years. I had stayed out late, I was excited I went down for tea and we watched TV. She lived around 20 min walk from the home so I said I'd walk there and back. When I left her house to go home, it was dark. She lived in a street of terraced houses. I walked to the end, turned the corner and you had to go under a railway bridge. There were no streetlights but I could see a shadow underneath the bridge as I was approaching it and it made me quite nervous. I crossed over to avoid the person but as soon as I got under the bridge, a man started walking towards me. He had a long black coat on. "Excuse me," he said, "have you got the time?" I shook my head. "No, sorry," I replied. "Hang on, wait there," he said, as he got nearer to me. My heart was pounding in my chest. "I've got to go, I'm going to be late," I said. He stood in front of me, opened his coat and he was naked but had clingfilm wrapped around his stomach and penis. "Help me get out of this, touch me!" I started screaming and managed to run past him. I ran all the way home, losing a shoe in the process. I was having a panic attack, tears streaming down my face, heart racing, I had pins and needles all over my body. I got to the home and was banging on the door for them to open it, still hysterical. Mavis came to the door, I fell into her arms, shaking all over. "What's happened?" she said. I couldn't tell her because I was crying too much. She pushed me off her and slapped me straight across the face to make me calm down. "A man," I said, "a man wrapped in clingfilm asking me to touch him under the bridge."

She sat me on the sofa and made me a cup of tea. "Now calm down because I can't understand what you're saying." She left me there for half an hour for me to get myself together. I calmly told her what had happened, and she rang the police. Nothing ever came of it, he wasn't found but it frightened me to the point where I never walked anywhere on my own again. There are so many disturbed people out there, it wasn't just my family. That is someone's son, maybe husband or even worse father that gets his kicks off flashing at young girls whilst wrapped in clingfilm. Flashers in the street, paedophiles as fathers – I'd like to think the world has changed for the better over time but unfortunately it has got worse, as I found out in my thirties.

I was on a night out with my friend. She had been staying at mine and I had been looking after her. I'd been having parties at my house, being stupid, taking drugs and basically being a complete knob head. I'm not proud of the way I behaved in my thirties, I'm quite ashamed of it. I had spurts where I was out of control and it didn't suit me. They weren't really parties – it was the same few people that used to come around sometimes we would drink, but when the kids went to their dads, we would be taking drugs and listening to music. One day one of the lads brought his mum's boyfriend with him. I took an instant dislike to him he was cocky, very sure of himself. I asked them not to bring him to my house again, he was Turkish and just glared at me, made me feel very uneasy in my own home. On that night out I saw him, he was wearing a white suit, something like Michael Jackson would have worn back in the day. He came over and asked if he could buy me a drink. I refused and walked away, a few hours later I saw him again and once again he was just glaring at me. When me and my friend went home, we were tipsy and ended up having an argument over money. I told her I couldn't pay for everything all the time, I got into bed and she left.

I fell asleep and woke up with him in my bed, kissing my breasts. I was screaming – get the fuck out of my house, what are you doing? – I wasn't even safe in my own home. I managed to get him out of the house. He was shouting at me, calm down, I thought you wanted me. At what point did I make him think I wanted him? I refused his drink, I didn't speak to him, in fact, I tried my best to avoid him because he creeped me out.

I had a dog flap in the kitchen and that's how he got into my house, I knew I couldn't have a shower, I knew the drill but I didn't want to ring the police. I was scared of what my friend would say – this was his mother's boyfriend. I went downstairs secured the house the best I could and just sat there staring at my door waiting for morning to come. As soon as it was light, I rang my friend and told him I needed to speak to him urgently. We arranged to meet. I was frightened going out of the house but went to meet him. When I got there, his uncle was with him. As soon as I opened my mouth, I started to cry. I told them both what had happened and told them I hadn't rung the police. I knew that what I was telling them was difficult and I knew it could potentially break up their family. They both told me I had to ring the police which was good to hear. I wanted justice. I was scared in my own home. I went home and rang the police. They came to my house – I wrote a statement and they took forensics and took my clothes. They went and arrested the Turkish man who denied even being at my home and until the forensics came back, it was my word against his. I was back in the situation again. I felt helpless, but confident this time there was DNA. There was forensics, surely, I was going to get justice. I wanted to go to court. I wanted to stand up in front of a jury and tell them what this sick bastard had done.

When the police finally came back to me, it was the news I had been longing for. He had been charged with sexual assault and entering without permission. He had denied everything but they found his DNA inside my bra, in my bed. The feeling of finally getting some justice for something someone had done to me – I was ecstatic. He went to the Magistrates' court and I found out he lived on the next street to me. I felt instantly panicked, the case was referred to the Crown court and he put a plea in of not guilty, which I was happy about, because I could have my day in court.

It took months to get to court and I had to move to a new house. I couldn't sleep. I didn't feel safe in my own home. I was a mess, I was frightened I was going to bump into him in the street. I was getting taxis 200 meters up the road and not turning in for work, so I had to move home. I had to for my mental health, I was losing the plot again. It did, however, stop me drinking and taking drugs. I didn't want anyone in my house and I wanted to be alert at all times. I remember walking into the Crown court that day and I was ready for him. They put me in witness protection upstairs, but I wasn't bothered. I wanted to come face to face with this man. I was worried about my friend turning up – she had been called as a witness. I hadn't spoken to her since it happened. I was angry with her for leaving. If she had stayed, he might not have attacked, but who knows? When I walked into witness protection, she was there. We both started crying – she told me she would never have let me down and not turned up and how sorry she was. We had a good talk and I was wrong to put the blame on her for all this time. It wasn't her fault at all. It was his, the dirty scumbag that thinks he can attack women in bed. To my surprise, the pervert's wife had stuck by him – he was pleading not guilty and she believed him, silly woman.

The barrister came in to talk to me about the case, told me he didn't know how long the trial would take because he was still saying not guilty. I wasn't bothered how long it took – it was going ahead – that's all that mattered to me. I was sat in the room all morning waiting for someone to come and get me, waiting for my day in court. They broke for lunch and I went downstairs for a cigarette and there he was. I just stared at him straight in the eye and he was still cocksure of himself smiling at me. I hate that man so much, he turned and walked away from me and I still just glared until he was out of sight. My blood was boiling. I wanted to scream at him, tell him what he had done to me, how he had left me empty and soulless, how he had ripped apart the final bit of hope I had in the human race.

After lunch, I was sat in the witness protection room and the barrister walked in smiling. "I have good news, Emma," he said, "he has changed his plea to guilty." "What does that mean?" I said. "It means you don't have to stand up in court, he will just get sentenced." Because he had changed his plea to guilty, he made a deal with the courts and got a two-year suspended sentence. No prison, not deported – I was furious. I wanted a trial, I wanted him to be found guilty, not just say he was, so he didn't have to go to prison. He walked out of court a free man and I was a prisoner in my own home. Why? I felt failed again. He could go back to his everyday life and I still have to live in fear of bumping into him. This was 8 years ago, and I still look for him in the streets when I'm walking on my own. I still dread bumping into him, another pervert who ruined me.

I was meant to keep in touch with my social worker until I was 18, but Francis didn't really help me. I never felt comfy talking to her. She used to pick me up from school once a fortnight and take me to the Little Chef. We only had an hour on my lunch break. By the time we drove there and had food, it was time to come back. I'd tell her I was OK and she would just smile and nod. It wasn't really a good relationship, but I looked forward to my burger and fries and loved the selection of dips that came with it in spinning silver dishes. I used to think the Little Chef was posh when I was a kid – it wasn't posh just expensive but never the less I would still like to go back one day and have my burger. It wasn't much but it is a good memory.

I ended up moving into the hostel with Tammy. I tried staying with my sister but it didn't really work out. I love my sister very much – both of my sisters – but I don't know them. I know their birthdays and the names of their children but I don't know details. We have never kept in touch. We don't speak and it upsets me when I think about it – all I've ever wanted was a family. It would be good to have someone to go to or catch up with. I'd like to know how they are, how their lives are going, if they're happy. I hope they're happy and I hope one day we could go out the three of us for a meal and talk. I need them to know what I have been through – they don't know the truth. They have never asked and I've never told them. It would be good to see them and be good for us all to get together. I'm going to make that happen one day.

The hostel was fun. We were living on our own. There were six of us and we were all young and free. I met some amazing people in there. The hostel was in a beautiful area, huge houses with a park facing. The residents hated us, and I lost count how many petitions went in to try and get the hostel closed down. Everything that went wrong in the area, the police were there. Cars stolen – it's the kids from the hostel. Burglaries – must be us! Even the local shoplifters must have lived with us. The police were there that many times, we got used to it. Truth was, there was me and Tammy, a guy who was lovely but had nowhere to go but had a good job and was very respectful, a punk girl who never came out of her room and had her door locked at all times and two brothers. OK, so the two brothers were a bit tasteful and had a history of petty theft and had spent their whole life in and out of care and young offenders' institutes but they were trying to change their life. But unfortunately, once tarnished with a brush, it's hard for people to believe in you and when your address is the only hostel in town that everyone is trying to shut down, it's hard getting ahead in life. They both dabbled in drugs and weren't given a break and continued with the life of crime.

I started working full-time in the café and spent most of my time there. I was earning £52 a week and ended up falling out with Tammy, a stupid argument over a boy. She knocked ten bells of shit out of me. I ended up with stitches in my eyebrows where she popped them. It was my own fault. She asked me to tell one of the lads in the hostel that she fancied him, and when I spoke to him, he told me he liked me. I went back into the room and lied to her, told her he liked her too and she found out. She was furious – I had broken our code. We had lived together like sisters for years and I lied to her over a boy and let her make a fool of herself. I ended up going back to my sister's and I didn't speak to her for 9 months. I wish I had – another regret I can't take back.

She ended up getting in a relationship with the eldest brother from the hostel. I believe they were so in love and I would have loved to have seen her finally happy and settled, but I never got the chance. Our stupid argument will stay with me forever. I was in work one day and my social worker walked in and asked if she could speak to me. She sat me down and told me Tammy had died in a car accident – she was in a stolen car with her friend and boyfriend and they lost control of the vehicle and it went into a tree. Three of them walked away unhurt and Tammy died instantly. I couldn't breathe – how had this happened? Should I have stayed? Would she have got in a stolen car if I was still there? I miss her still and think about our time in care together from time to time. I would not have got through those years without her. She was a massive part of my life. It's thirty years since she passed but I know she will be happy up there with her mum. It all got too much for her boyfriend, too. He died a couple of years later of a drug overdose, a waste of a beautiful person with the cheekiest smile I have ever seen.

He wasn't a bad kid, he needed what we all needed – to be loved. He found it and was heartbroken when Tammy died – a piece of him died that day too.

I remember going to see him at the hostel and they had huge windows you could pull up. He was sat on the window ledge staring up at the sky listening to *All About Eve* by Martha's Harbour. A beautiful song and it will always remind me of that moment. I've not heard about the other brother – we had a brief relationship whilst we were in the hostel. I hope he's doing OK and made something of himself. It would be good to hear that he has. Actually, it'd be good to see him again, see how he is, but thirty years is a long time who knows where people are and what they're doing?

7:

On the Mend

When I started writing this, I was a broken woman, I was in a place I never want to go back to. I was weak, exposed, confused. I had no idea what was happening to me and I spent three months trying to build myself back up. I pushed everyone away I couldn't talk to anyone. I was reliant on medication to numb all the thoughts. They tried me on all sorts of medicines and finally settled me on anti-psychotic medicines that are used to treat schizophrenia. When I first started taking them, I was having fifty dreams a night, all real things that had happened. It was releasing my backlog of memories as I slept, or rather didn't sleep. I was waking up after every dream, crying, not understanding why I was re-living my childhood as I slept.

Before I started taking medicine, I was awake for days on end, staring at my ceiling, frightened to close my eyes, thinking someone was going to come and attack me. So, although I was re-living everything, it was clearing my head and I was starting to get some rest. I never spoke to anyone, just lay on my bed, holding myself, trying to comfort myself. I have been on and off anti-depressants all my life, but this time was different. I was a different person. I didn't recognise the person who looked back at me, I had constant thoughts of death. I wanted to end my life but didn't want to put that on my children. I was frightening myself with this darkness. I was seeing everything that had happened to me because of my medication. but not one experience at a time. My whole life just there constantly – it wouldn't go away. The fingers pushing inside me, in my princess dress and Michael Pyre's face with those big thick-rimmed black glasses, smirking at me with his tiny head and his old wrinkled hands. Dirty hands, dirty fingernails inside my vagina, but it wasn't just him. The animals, the spastic, the girls, the dicks, the breasts, the evil. I wore a red satin dress. I was the devil, the dirty horrible devil that didn't deserve to be here. I didn't deserve a place in society.

I could feel the sick in the back of my throat, from the dicks getting shoved down it. I could feel the wiry pubic hairs scratching my legs, see the cat's eyes staring at me. It was 24-hour torture of myself and I couldn't stop it. It wouldn't go away, I had to go to Dave and Brenda's every day for the crisis team to come and see me. I saw someone for an hour or two, every day for two months. On a couple of occasions, they would leave the room and ring the big boss for advice because I was a mess. I would just sit and cry. I couldn't explain what was happening in my head, it was too painful. I would just sit and cry. You get to see a lot of different people every day especially the support workers so going over the same things with different people, I couldn't do it. I didn't want to talk about the same things, I wanted to try and move forward, so I would just sit and cry and when they had gone, I'd sit with Brenda. I owe her so much. The support she and Dave gave me. They now call me their adopted daughter which makes me smile because you couldn't ask for better people to call Mum and Dad. Mentally, physically, emotionally, they were there one hundred per cent. I could say anything, and they would love me unconditionally. I'd write at night time and go over the next day and let them read what I had written so they could support me, and they have not stopped since. They have been my shoulder, my support and most definitely my rock.

After a couple of weeks of the crisis team, they sent me a psychologist called David and he got me on the road to recovery. He did exercises to do with my mental state, made me see what was happening to me. But more importantly, we put together a letter in my words, to give my children to try and help them understand what had happened to me. This was very difficult – writing my feelings down when I'd never told them things. Letting them see me completely stripped back. I've never shown the kids that letter. I thought about it, but it was an outline. It was a diagnosis – it wasn't what had happened and for the first time, I needed them to know everything, to try and understand who I was and where I had come from.

I've now sent them all the first chapter of this book and I think they've all started to understand. I will be there to support them and answer any questions they may have because I am able to do that now where I could never have done it before. I remember my son looking at me back in March – it was a look of disgust. He couldn't handle seeing me the way I was, and I couldn't tell him why I was too weak. When he read my first chapter he came to me, hugged me and said, "Mum, I had never seen you like that and I got angry. I didn't know what to do. I thought you were weak because of a man and it angered me. I have learnt everything from you. I have learnt to survive, to fight, to graft all because of you. You made me strong and to see you like that and I thought it was over a man, it tore me apart."

I got that, my son has been to hell and back and he has fought every step of the way and I have been by his side, every step of it. All my children have had really bad problems. They have all, at some point in their lives, been given a bad hand, but I'm not going to talk about that now. I have had to be strong for them their whole lives and at times I have failed them, I know I have. Especially my eldest, in my times of despair I wasn't there for her and looking back, I should have been. All of my kids have needed me at some point and because I found it difficult to talk, I used to brush things away. I don't want to be that person anymore. I want to support them all and I have a great relationship with each and every one of them now. And I hope I can always cheer them up when they're at their lowest and encourage them to keep fighting. I love them all from the bottom of my heart.

Letting go of this will not only benefit me, but them too. It will make me stronger to be there for them and I hope they know that I will try my best for them every day and will love them unconditionally until I take my last breath. After six months of trying to get my head together, I had to leave my job. I was ashamed of who I was, embarrassed, and I didn't want people's opinion of me to change. I'd got myself in a bad financial situation, being off work, my savings were gone and I was adding more pressure to myself by trying to deal with my money worries as well.

I had my final visit with the main psychiatrist who told me that I had killed the gas in my head from storing memories. He said I had stored so much to try to forget it, that the memory part of my brain had shut down and at that point, I had broken. It was the tipping point – the rejection I felt over my break up. My brain couldn't cope with it and I tipped, and everything came flooding back. Post-Traumatic Stress Disorder – I've still not learnt about it, but I know I can't use that as an excuse to not keep fighting. I was in the dark about PTSD – I thought it was something only soldiers had. What I went through was traumatic and it had and probably will have a lasting effect on my life. Only this time, instead of storing it, I'm talking about it, dealing with it, which is the best therapy for me. It's out in the open – I'm telling everyone how I felt, the urges I had, the things I did, so I can't hide from it anymore.

After I'd been writing for a couple of months, Dave and Brenda suggested I sent this over to a couple of their friends who live in France and have connections in the writing world. At first, I was afraid. I was writing this for me. I was releasing it for my mental health, but then I thought what if I could get this out there and help someone who has either been through a similar upbringing or knows someone who is trying to deal with it. Or what if I could help the children of people who have been abused to try and understand the emotion and torment we put ourselves through, so I sent it. This resulted in me having a visit to France in September – that was two months ago. I have just had my 46th birthday on 22nd November and I want to finish this on where I am today.

A lot has happened in 9 months and if I look back to the beginning of the year and where I am now, I impress myself. France was the turning point. We booked to go on the ferry because Dave and Brenda were taking me as I was going to meet their friends. Brenda is scared of flying so the ferry was our only option. We were going to Le Barde which is in the country and an hour from Bordeaux. A two-week holiday in the country – Dave and Brenda warned me of the tranquillity and that there wasn't much to do. Our itinerary for when we got there consisted of fishing, rowing, walking and cycling. My kids laughed when I told them and said it was going to be the longest and worst two-week holiday I have ever been on and I must admit I wasn't excited to go. In fact, I was dreading it – don't get me wrong, I love to holiday – but I've only ever been on party holidays. Dave and Brenda used to live in France and were just across a river from the people we were going to see.

Our journey started with a trip down to Portsmouth – a five-hour drive from where we were, but Brenda has family there, so to break up our journey we headed down in the morning and were going to go and have a meal and a few drinks at her family's home. We arrived – they have a beautiful home and I was made to feel welcome immediately. I'm generally not very good at meeting new people, unless I'm in work mode but straight away I felt at ease. More family and friends came and what started as a quiet afternoon turned into a lovely gathering and the wine was flowing. We were only fifteen minutes from the docks, so we asked Brenda what time we had to be there. We were sailing at 10.30pm, so we decided to leave at half nine. Brenda had a bit too much of the vino and fell asleep on the sofa.

We were travelling from Portsmouth to San Malo which is an 11-hour ferry crossing, so with a cabin booked, we could have a good sleep overnight as we still had a five-hour drive the other end. We got in the car and drove to the port. When we got there, Brenda was still asleep in the back of the car, so I leant around and got the documents out of the seat pocket where she kept everything. I opened the documents, looked at Dave and said, "Dave, we've missed the ferry." "Don't be silly," he said, "it's only 9pm, we left early." I said, "Yes,

I know but the ferry went at 8.30pm," and showed him the paperwork.

We didn't know whether to laugh or cry – we both just sat there staring at each other. We went into the office and yes, we had missed it, but they could get us on another ferry at 11pm, however, we wouldn't be going to the same port and we couldn't have a cabin. By this point, me and Dave could not control our laughter. We settled for the journey, so we sat in the port for another two hours. We got on the ferry and headed straight for the bar, got a round of drinks and then they called last orders. For 11 hours, we sat on the ferry, with no drinks in the most uncomfortable chairs you could imagine. It was an experience. We ended up in Caen. Back in the car, we looked at the map – another eight and a half-hour drive. I felt so sorry for Dave by the time we got there. He was exhausted, but he was a great sport the whole way and all we did was laugh. It's not a journey I would recommend, however, we did manage to make it back on the right ferry at the right time.

When we arrived in Le Barde I instantly felt the isolation. It certainly was in the country. We were staying in a house Dave had built when he lived there and after swearing never to return to France they had done it because of me. To be staying in a house he had built must have been even harder.

When we go to the house, it was beautiful. The sun was full-blaze in the sky – perfect, I thought. Then I realised I had no Wi-Fi, no 4G, no music, no television – what on earth was I going to do for two weeks? Oh yeah, walk, I thought, sarcastically. Later that night we went to their friends' house for dinner and from that moment I fell in love. I have no idea what happened to me in those two weeks, but it was the best holiday of my life. When I mentioned being free as a child in the garden – well it was like that, but on a much larger scale. I did go walking and cycling, and sightseeing. I did row a boat down the river and I went to the most beautiful places. All day you got the feeling of tranquillity and open space and at night time too.

Most nights we went to the friends and they made dinner and we sat outside and talked. It was surreal. On the first night there, all the three streetlights that were near us went off, so everywhere was pitch black. I've never seen such darkness. We got chairs and sat in the middle of the garden, being careful the geckos didn't run up my leg. Dave had a torch on. "Now sit down," he said, "and look up to the sky." He turned off the torch and wow the sky was a blanket of stars. You could see everything – it was the most beautiful thing I have ever seen. We sat for hours most nights, just talking and looking at the sky. I tried to take a picture of its beauty, but it was something you can only see with a human eye. I can't wait to go back to do it all again. Brenda and Dave's friends are two of the nicest people I have ever met. I felt a part of them by the time I was coming back, and I was so emotional to leave I didn't want to go. I wanted to stay longer – two weeks was not enough.

Next time I go back I am going to go for longer, to experience that feeling, to have no anxiety, to feel completely at peace with myself. I learnt a lot about myself in those two weeks. I was strong again, I was a different woman. In fact, I was stronger than I was before I had my breakdown I felt good about myself. I can't remember ever feeling good about myself. When I was leaving France, I put my hands over the top of my head and pretended to pull out all the crap that I had in it. I threw it on the floor before I got on the ferry. None of that is coming home with me, I thought to myself.

I got on that ferry a new woman, but it didn't last very long. A couple of months later, I reverted back to self-loathing. Finding fault in every inch of me. Blaming myself for everything that was happening. Dating people that can't show love because that's what I can handle that's what I'm used to. They will always fail because I want so much to be loved. I want someone to strip me apart, layer by layer and see vulnerable me, but I know that's never going to happen because I need to work on myself. I need to like who I am and stop blaming myself.

Almost two years since my breakdown and I have enrolled myself in a mental health group and after a few discussions, they have said I need long term therapy which I'm OK with. I need to stay single, work on myself and hopefully find peace within. I've been doing this for 45 years now, it's time for a change. I have tried to come off my medication, but doctors have told me – it's not for my mental health, it's for my brain. Now I know I will have to take it for life. I guess I had to have the breakdown. I had to open Pandora's Box.

As for Craig, I still have a glimmer of hope. A few months ago, I spoke to his sister over Facebook. She told me what he had done to them since she was a baby and how she only knew how to touch like me. She has turned to religion and vowed to me that when her mum dies – Craig's mum – she is going to go to the police and report him. Her and her sister – they are going to tell them everything. She won't do it until she dies though, because she still looks after Ben and she doesn't want to hurt her mum. I get that. I tried protecting my mum and she is a twat, so I understand her wanting to protect a woman who's been there for her throughout her whole life. Right now, at this moment in time, my life is OK. My kids are happy, I have good friends, I'm enjoying my work, and I am finally working on myself. Just one more wish – that I get the icing on the cake and Jane and Susan do come forward and I hope that vile creature finally gets what he deserves. Prison.

———————

Acknowledgements

Jarred, thank you for your hard work and confidentiality.

Beth and Jeremy not only are you two of the nicest, kindest people to grace this earth but without your belief and support, I don't think I would have ever finished this. Thank you for everything you have done.

Dave and Brenda! I would not have made it through my breakdown without you. You have treated me much more than a friend. It may have taken 47 years, but you have shown me not only how it feels to receive unconditional love, but how it feels to have a mum and dad. I owe my life to you both. I love you.

My children, a mother's love should never end, and I will love you with my last breath. I may not be proud of some of the things in my life, but you are my greatest achievement. I am so lucky to have kind, caring, beautiful children inside and out and I thank each one of you for all the love and support you have given me when I needed it most. I love you so much.

Leah and Lincoln thank you for being so perfect you have put a smile on my face and in my heart.

*Available worldwide from Amazon
and all good bookstores*

---

www.mtp.agency

www.facebook.com/mtp.agency

@mtp_agency